"I play Buddy Holly every night before I go on — it keeps me honest!"

—**Bruce Springsteen**

"Looking back over the last 20 years, I guess the guy I've admired most in rock 'n' roll is Buddy Holly."

—**Elvis Presley**

"The music of the late '50s and early '60s... that for me is meaningful music. The songs and musicians I grew up with transcend nostalgia — Buddy Holly and Johnny Ace are just as valid to me today as then."

—**Bob Dylan**

"Everything Buddy did he did with a sense of urgency that he wasn't going to have a lot of time... I think it was because he was doing what he wanted to do more than anything."

—**Larry Holley**
(Buddy's brother)

"When he was on stage he worked real hard and got through to the kids. He would tear up the audience.

—**Tommy Allsup**
(Guitarist with Holly and the Crickets)

"Marty Robbins also thinks Buddy has what it takes...."

—**Eddie Crandall 12/2/55**
(Marty Robbins' manager who took Buddy Holly's first masters to his first record company, Decca)

"The only thing I was given credit for — probably the most accurate thing I've ever been given credit for — was being a keen observer. I didn't create anything. Buddy was the creator... I left the mold fluid, let Buddy set his own mold. So i was able to capture on tape what Buddy created as an artist."

—**Norman Petty**

"But something touched me deep inside the day the music died...."

—**Don McLean**
from his song "American Pie"

Words by Don McLean
Copyright © 1971, 1972 MAYDAY MUSIC, INC. & THE BENNY BIRD CO.
International Copyright Secured   All Rights Reserved

buddy HOLLY

Songs • Photos • Stories

Golden Anniversary Songbook

Published by
MPL COMMUNICATIONS, INC.

Exclusively distributed by
HAL LEONARD PUBLISHING CORPORATION

Compiled & Edited by RONNY S. SCHIFF
Graphic design by ELYSE MORRIS WYMAN

Front cover + pages 3, 72(b) FLAIR PHOTOGRAPHY; 1 HARRY HAMMOND; 6, 7, 9, 13, 14, 18, 35, 56, 64, 89, 101 + back cover JOHN BEECHER COLLECTION; 8, 10, 12, 19, 20(b), 34, 36(b), 37(b), 55, 87, 111(t), 111(b) J I ALLISON; 11, 64, 89(b) ELLA HOLLEY; 17, 73(b) SPORT & GENERAL; 36(t) VI PETTY; 71 JOHN BEECHER; 88 STEVE BONNER.

Copyright © 1986 MPL COMMUNICATIONS, INC.
International Copyright Secured
All Rights Reserved   Made in U.S.A.

All rights in this book are reserved. No part of the book may be used or reproduced in any manner whatsoever without written permission.
ISBN 0-88188-557-6

Golden Anniversary Songbook

SONGS • PHOTOS • STORIES

CONTENTS

AN EMPTY CUP (And A Broken Date)	47
EVERYDAY	31
FOOL'S PARADISE	78
HEARTBEAT	92
I'M GONNA LOVE YOU TOO	60
I'M LOOKIN' FOR SOMEONE TO LOVE	24
IT'S SO EASY	82
LAST NIGHT	52
LISTEN TO ME	65
LONESOME TEARS	84
LOOK AT ME	68
LOVE'S MADE A FOOL OF YOU	104
MAYBE BABY	58
MOONDREAMS	98
NOT FADE AWAY	42
OH BOY!	38
PEGGY SUE	28
PEGGY SUE GOT MARRIED	96
RAVE ON	74
ROCK ME MY BABY	50
TAKE YOUR TIME	76
THAT'LL BE THE DAY	22
TRUE LOVE WAYS	102
WELL ALL RIGHT	90
WHAT TO DO	106
WORDS OF LOVE	26
YOU'VE GOT LOVE	44
DISCOGRAPHY	108

Buddy Holly's Story

Buddy Holly was born in Lubbock, Texas on September 7, 1936 and named Charles Hardin Holley after his grandfathers. The nickname Buddy was given him when his parents decided his "was too long a name for such a little boy." The "Holly" spelling came about from an uncorrected mistake on Buddy's first recording contract.

The Holleys were a musical family — playing for fun with Mrs. Ella Holley accompanying everyone on piano. Buddy studied violin for a short time and then took up piano for nine months. Piano was replaced almost immediately by steel guitar and finally by acoustic guitar. His parents always obliged these instrument changes by providing the new instrument and the lessons!

Holly played very well by ear, had a great rhythmic "feel" and by the sixth grade was proficient enough to regale his schoolmates with his playing in a Hank Williams style.

In 1949 at Hutchison Jr. High in Lubbock, Holly met Bob Montgomery who also played guitar and sang country tunes. They joined together, fashioning themselves after the Louvin Brothers and Johnnie and Jack, popular country bluegrass duos of the time. Between 1950 and 1952, they performed in high school talent shows and at local clubs, with Bob usually singing lead. In 1953, Larry Welborn a bassist, joined them.

Holly's and Montgomery's musical tastes expanded quite rapidly in their teen years. Lubbock, being somewhat geographically isolated from its closest big city neighbors, had the benefit of many visiting groups of rock and country artists, since they were able to draw substantial crowds. The schools were extremely supportive of their music programs and the local radio stations often sponsored country jamborees where hometown artists could perform and compete for prizes. These factors and the heaviest influence of all, *radio,* contributed a variety of styles to the duo's music education — bluegrass, country, blues, rock and rhythm and blues (which they picked up from a station in Louisiana!).

This particular melange of styles is what molded Holly's rockabilly style. John Goldrosen ("Buddy Holly: His Life And Music"/Popular Press) notes also that it was a natural progression for country performers to move into rock or rockabilly since country music was *dance* music and country vocalists acted as lead singers for small rhythm groups, which was the way rock was evolving in the early '50s. By 1953, the "Buddy and Bob Show" dubbed their music "Western and Bop."

The nation's first all-country radio station, KDAV, in Lubbock (daytime hours only initially) gave Buddy's and Bob's career a real boost when they were given a regular half-hour slot on the 2:30 pm, "Sunday Party." Holly even interjected some R&B into their act — like country music, it

Early publicity photo 1955

Early publicity photo 1956

was music with a beat. As rock 'n' roll grew in '54, Holly added even more R&B and their show became a live attraction for teens. By 1955, they were getting requests to sing Elvis Presley songs and the country-rock sound was firmly established.

Getting a record deal was the important next step and the duo cut several demos in 1954 and 1955 (these were released in 1965 as the album "HOLLY IN THE HILLS"), however no record company interest was forthcoming. Interest came when Buddy and Bob were the openers for a KDAV-sponsored show starring Bill Haley and the Comets. Eddie Crandall, Marty Robbins' manager booked the show and was impressed with Holly. He wrote Dave Stone, owner of KDAV, saying he was "...confident that I can do something as far as getting Buddy Holly a recording contract." He asked Stone to have Holly make four demos with the admonishment "...don't change his style at all."

The demos went several routes in Nashville, one finding its way to Jim Denny, a talent agent, who sparked the interest of Paul Cohen from Decca Records. By mid-January 1956, Holly was offered a contract, but with one hitch — Bob Montgomery was not included. Holly didn't want to sign, but Montgomery convinced him this was the opportunity of a lifetime and to take it.

The tracks from the three sessions done in Nashville for Decca were not released until 1958 as *"THAT'LL BE THE DAY"* and re-released in 1967 as *"THE GREAT BUDDY HOLLY."* Various top Nashville studio players were in on these sessions including Grady Martin, Boots Randolph and Sonny Curtis. Drummer Jerry Allison, still in high school, sat in for a session as well.

Decca released two singles in '56, both reviewed favorably in the music trades, but they did not do well with the public. Part of the problem was a "fish or fowl" situation — too rock 'n' roll for country stations and not enough rock 'n' roll for rock stations. By the end of '56 it was obvious to Holly that Decca was not going to renew his contract.

Holly's next fortuitous stop was Clovis, New Mexico at the studios of Norman Petty. Petty, an independent producer and artist in his own right, had several pop hits including his own tune *"Almost Paradise."* He also had fine recording equipment, excellent connections with the New York music business and a good ear for commercial pop and rock music. Holly re-recorded *"That'll Be The Day"* (see the "Song Stories" beginning on page 19) along with several other tunes in that early portion of 1957 with Jerry Allison on drums, Larry Welborn initially on bass who was

Buddy Holly, Jerry Allison, Bob Montgomery, July 1956

then replaced by Joe Mauldin, Niki Sullivan on rhythm guitar and various studio backup singers.

Petty took the demos to the publishing company, Peer-Southern, who handled his music, and their ever-astute Murray Deutsch took the demos to Bob Thiele, a producer for Coral Records, a subsidiary of Decca (both of these men continue to be powers in the music business). Thiele liked what he heard so much, he signed them to the Coral/Brunswick label after securing Holly's release from the parent company, and used the master of *"That'll Be*

Recording for Decca in Nashville, November 1956

The Day" as Holly's first release. Allison, Sullivan and Mauldin (just fresh out of high school) became Holly's regular band, the Crickets (see "Song Story" on *"I'm Gonna Love You Too"* for origin of Crickets' name). *

The Crickets' name only was on the first release *"That'll Be The Day,"* which came out on the Brunswick label. Billboard gave it a somewhat favorable review, labeling it "medium beat rockabilly," and saying that the "...performance is better than material." By September, the song was enormous hit!

To double the band's potential, Petty, who was now the band's manager, came up with the concept of separate releases for Holly and the Crickets. Holly's first release *"Words Of Love"* did not do well (see page 19), but his second solo effort was *"Peggy Sue."* The Crickets' were released on Brunswick, Holly on Coral...a good marketing move, since DJ's were more likely to play records by different groups at the same time. There was little distinction between the Holly and Crickets recordings as far as rhythm or style, however Holly's did not have additional vocal backups.

* Complete background on each song in this book can be found in the "Song Stories" portions.

Most of Holly's recordings were made late at night or early in the morning, when there was little activity in the studio. Petty's studio even had a couple of beds, and the group camped out there, rather than driving back and forth to Lubbock. His songs were usually formed melody first with the concept for the lyric molding the mood of the music. He was known to take a ride and come back with a fully-formed song. However, many times the Crickets figured in the final polishing of the songs.

With fans clamoring to see these new hitmakers, Holly and the Crickets were booked for Alan Freed's "Great Holiday Rock 'n' Roll Concerts" in New York over Labor Day weekend and then in the fall of '57 with the "Biggest Show Of Stars" tour. And, indeed, they were playing with the biggest stars — Fats Domino, Chuck Berry, Paul Anka, Clyde McPhatter, Frankie Lymon — on an 80 day tour that provided them with even more fans. It was during a break on this tour that their first Lp, *"THE CHIRPING CRICKETS"* was completed (see page 57).

On the way to Clovis, New Mexico for first session with Norman Petty

An unusual "glassesless" publicity pose — note Holly's stylish pegged pants and heavily-padded shoulders

"*Oh Boy!*" was released and hit the charts in November and by December both it and "*Peggy Sue*" were flying high. Two guest appearances on the Ed Sullivan show gave the group maximum national exposure, and Christmas found them back in New York playing Alan Freed's holiday shows at the Paramount. Allison remembered this as a time also when the Everly Brothers took the group to a store in New York for "fancy" clothes to get them out of their loud, huge suits or their standard "uniform" of tee-shirts, jeans and moccasins. Niki Sullivan left the group at this time.

Holly and the Crickets' records were selling well overseas and in February '57 they joined Paul Anka and Jerry Lee Lewis for a tour to Australia. The tour was a smash, the Aussies liked their "demeanor" and they left behind a large group of fans.

But the most enthusiastic fans were waiting in the U.K. and in March, Holly and the Crickets hit England for a 25 day tour. The tour was a rousing success. Melody Maker, England's biggest music publication, and New Musical Express praised their performances. They performed on television including BBC's "Off The Record" and their concerts were such hits that they ended up having four singles on the charts during one week ("*Peggy Sue*," "*Oh Boy!*," "*Maybe Baby*" and "*Listen To Me*").

"Maybe Baby" was released in the U.S. in February under the Crickets' name and became almost as big a hit as "Oh Boy!." Holly's second release "Listen To Me" didn't do quite as well in the U.S., but his third, "Rave On" released in April 1958 was a smash in both countries.

Back in the U.S. meant back on the tour route once again with Alan Freed. In June, Holly recorded without the other Crickets for the first time since the band was formed: while in New York, he cut two Bobby Darin tunes, "Early In The Morning" with a flip side of "Now We're One" which hit the charts by mid-summer and showed his versatility with a rhythm and blues/gospel style.

Branching in still another direction, Holly cut demos of two songs written with old partner Bob Montgomery aimed at other artists. Tommy Allsup played lead guitar at these sessions and Holly asked him to join the group making it once more a foursome, and making it possible for Holly to stop overdubbing his lead on their recordings.

New York in June 1958 brought about one other wonderful change in Holly's life, he fell in love. The story goes that he walked into his publisher's, Peer-Southern, office, met the receptionist Maria Elena Santiago and immediately asked her out to lunch. While at lunch with Petty and the Crickets, Holly announced to everyone, "You see this girl? I'm going to marry her..." On the next day, on their next date, Holly did propose and Maria Elena accepted, and on August 15th, 1958 they were married at the senior Holley's home in Lubbock. Jerry Allison had married the now-famous Peggy Sue and the four of them honeymooned in Acapulco. Afterwards Buddy and Maria Elena settled in Greenwich Village, feeling that remaining in the city was best for Holly's career.

In September, Holly extended himself in still another direction — as a record producer for Waylon Jennings' first recording. Jennings, a Lubbock DJ and country singer, cut a Cajun tune "Jole Blon" at a session set up, produced and financed by Holly. The famed R&B sax player, King Curtis was in on this session, during which

Fall 1957, on tour

January 1958, a new publicity still

Holly himself cut two tunes, *"Reminiscing"* by Curtis and *"Come Back Baby"* written by Norman Petty and Fred Neil. These cuts were not released until several years after Holly's death; the Curtis cut is noted for Holly's vocal stylization matching his voice to Curtis' sax sound.

Holly surprised everyone, especially Norman Petty, by expressing the desire to do a session with strings. Petty had been pushing to expand Holly's audience from rock to the wider pop area, and happily set up the session in mid-October. Four songs were cut, and *"It Doesn't Matter Anymore"/"Raining In My Heart"* was released in January 1959, a short time before Holly's death. *"It Doesn't Matter Anymore,"* written by Paul Anka and given to Holly the day of his recording session, did well on the U.S. charts and was Holly's biggest hit in the U.K., staying number one for six weeks.

During this time, the Crickets released *"It's So Easy"* which did not chart, followed by *"Think It Over"* which did hit the charts; while Holly's next release *"Heartbeat"* had only minor success. Then, toward the end of fall, Holly broke his association with Norman Petty. The

Publicity stills made late 1958 to promote Holly after his break with Norman Petty

Crickets, in turn, decided to stay with Petty. Although Holly went solo and wanted the independence, he did want the Crickets to rejoin him and told them they were welcome whenever they changed their minds.

Holly split from Petty, for the most part, because Petty's management "know-how" probably wasn't keeping up with Holly's popularity and because of some of the monies were just not forthcoming quickly enough. Maria Elena was extremely savy of music business practices and was energetic and supportive of Buddy's career. She helped set up fan clubs, started promotional activities rolling and had a score of new promo photos taken of him.

Toward the end of '58, Holly was filled with plans: He wanted to do an album with Ray Charles, he was taking Spanish guitar lessons, he wanted to produce other artists, he was even taking acting lessons with Maria Elena at the Lee Strasberg School of Method Acting. All of these plans needed bankrolling, and Holly agreed, once more, to go out on tour with GAC's "Winter Dance Party"; three weeks through the midwest in the heart of winter.

A new band was formed for the tour with Waylon Jennings on electric bass, Tommy Allsup on guitar and Charlie Bunch on drums, but Holly still missed the "magic" of playing with the Crickets on tour. In addition to Holly, there were only four other acts on this tour: Ritchie Valens whose hit *"Donna"* was at the top of the charts, J.P. "The Big Bopper" Richardson of *"Chantilly Lace"* fame, Dion and the Belmonts and Frankie Sardo.

Since they were married, Maria Elena had toured with Holly in their recently purchased, comfortable Cadillac. However since she was pregnant, Maria Elena decided to skip this tour and Holly would go on the bus with the other artists. A bus trip that was grueling at best and nightmarish most of the time (drummer Charlie Bunch suffered frostbite on the bus when the heat went out).

By the evening of February 2 the group had reached the resort town of Clear Lake, Iowa to play at the Surf Ballroom. Holly, Jennings and Allsup had had enough "bus" and chartered a plane to leave immediately after the concert and take them to Moorhead, Minnesota. There they could sleep in a hotel and take care of their accumulated laundry...luxuries after one-nighters on the bus.

When the Big Bopper came down with the flu Jennings relinquished his seat on the plane to him. Richie Valens bugged Allsup all evening to trade places, and Allsup decided the trade on a flip of a coin, provided he could use the Boppers' new sleeping bag on the bus!

Shortly after midnight on February 3rd, the plane left Mason City Airport with Holly, Valens and Richardson and pilot Roger Peterson. The weather was marginal with light snow flurries and Peterson was not instrument-rated. Jerry Dwyer, owner of the air service, watched the plane take off and sink slowly into the horizon — this he thought was a nighttime optical illusion. He was disturbed by the fact that Peterson had not filed a flight plan after take-off, and by early morning when no airports had heard anything from the plane, he began searching. He found the wreckage only eight miles from the field...everyone was dead.

Tragically, on the night of the crash, Jerry Allison and Joe Mauldin had tried to reach Holly to tell him they wanted to put the group back together.

The greatest commendation of an artist's work lies in the continuing popularity of his or her music and the influences on other artists to come.

Holly's lyric was straight-forward, always in tune with young people's feelings everywhere, in every generation. His music was his unique rockabilly combination of styles that had tremendous influence over the structure of many people's songs. His delivery, his sound was what tied it together; the sheer joy he took in performing and doing *anything* concerned with music shines through in his voice.

Everyone who remembers Holly, remembers him with warmth for the giving and exuberant person that he was. The books and articles written about him (especially John Goldrosen's "Buddy Holly: His Life And Music") pay deep and loving tribute to him and his music. Holly's songs continue to be recorded, new collections of his tracks are periodically released and the influence of his music can be seen throughout each musical era and with the greatest of great artists including the Beatles, the Rolling Stones and Bruce Springsteen!

Buddy Holly's Music

by Fred Sokolow

Buddy Holly played lead guitar on all the classic CRICKETS records. His lead breaks are crisp, original, playful and unique rockabilly gems that most '60s and '70s and '80s rock guitarists have studied and imitated. Like his vocalizing (which was equally influential in rock and roll history), Holly's guitar playing was a blend of country/western music and rhythm and blues.

In Lubbock, Texas, where Holly grew up, everyone listened to pop and country music; that's what was on the radio in the mid-'50s. Holly and his long-time musical partner, friend and drummer Jerry Allison were "into all the black music — like Clyde McPhatter, the Drifters and Ray Charles." In order to hear R&B, Allison recalls that he and Holly tuned in a late night radio broadcast from Shreveport — a thousand miles from Lubbock. Thus Holly absorbed the guitar sounds of people like T-Bone Walker, B.B. King and other black early-to-mid '50s, single-note-style, electric guitarists.

Elvis was another big influence. Before Holly made any hit records he performed and recorded with a fiddler/guitarist named Sonny Curtis. Curtis could play all the Scotty Moore guitar licks from Elvis' early records; Holly admired Curtis' playing and probably learned some rockabilly technique from him. Around 1955 Holly met Elvis and shared a bill with him in Lubbock. He then went through a phase of imitating Elvis' singing and doing all his repertoire. He even temporarily dropped the drummer from his act because Elvis played without a drummer in Lubbock.

Buddy Holly evolved his own guitar sound in endless jam sessions with Jerry Allison. In 1955, Allison's drums were set up in Holly's parents' living room, and the two tried every musical idea that came into their heads. They also performed as a duo. Allison says: "He and I used to play dances — not even a bass player, and he would play chord lead. He wouldn't play just single string things like was normal — that was the most different thing about the whole Buddy Holly and the Crickets thing — what Buddy played on the guitar. We had to fill up all the holes in the music."

The chording solos Allison spoke of can be heard on some of Holly's biggest hits: his lead breaks on *"Peggy Sue"* and *"Not Fade Away"* were all chords and no single notes. These tunes were recorded in 1957 at Norman Petty's studio in Clovis, New Mexico, where so many of Holly's best records were produced. Other tunes the Crickets recorded in Clovis — which were released after Holly's death — reveal the diverse influences on his guitar style. He played a Bo Diddley-style chord lead in the song *"Bo Diddley,"* and a Chuck Berryesque lead in Berry's *"Brown-Eyed Handsome Man."* Other tracks display a hard-driving rockabilly style that blends Chuck Berry double-note licks, chordal lead and Scotty Moore-like finger-picking licks. By 1957 Holly had a style of his own. *That'll Be The Day,"* "*Oh Boy!"* and other hits recorded in Clovis have lead breaks that combined all the country, R&B and rockabilly influences in a unique and fresh way. He peppered his solos with playful guitaristic ideas like half-muted strings and boogie-woogie bass patterns; his guitar sound became recognizable and personal.

Holly was also a very inventive recording artist and broke new ground in the studio during those early rock years. Norman Petty gave him free reign and charged the Crickets "per tune" instead of "per hour," so the band was often up past dawn perfecting a track. According to Petty, "Buddy was in the studio all the time. I was recording other people at the time too, but it would have suited him fine if I had just dropped everything and just recorded Buddy. He would have been there twenty-four hours a day."

Holly double-tracked vocal and guitar parts on *"Words Of Love"* by a process of trial-and-error (because this was never done at the time). On *"Peggy Sue"* he had the drums removed from the studio and run through an echo device; then he manually raised and lowered the volume in time with the music, for an unusual effect. Petty recalls that while Holly was running down *"Everyday"* for the band, "Jerry (Allison) started to join in, improvising by slapping his knees, and the sound appealed to Holly. So the only drumming on the recording is Jerry Allison slapping his knees."

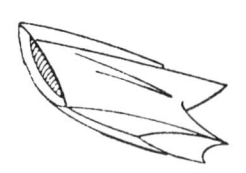

To show how primitive recording conditions were in those days, Crickets' rhythm guitarist Niki Sullivan recalls recording *Peggy Sue:* "Buddy couldn't switch from rhythm to lead fast enough without breaking rhythm. He couldn't get his hand to the switch fast enough and it showed up on tape. So we stopped and redid it with me pushing the switch on Buddy's guitar."

The enthusiasm of the Crickets, the freshness of their approach, makes their records shine. Holly loved playing and recording, and he found ways to turn the studio's limitations into assets: there was so much to be learned, so many new things to invent. It was an exciting time for rock guitar, too, with R&B, country/western and rockabilly styles all fusing to form a new rock and roll sound. And nobody played the new style guitar music with more freshness, taste and drive than Buddy Holly.

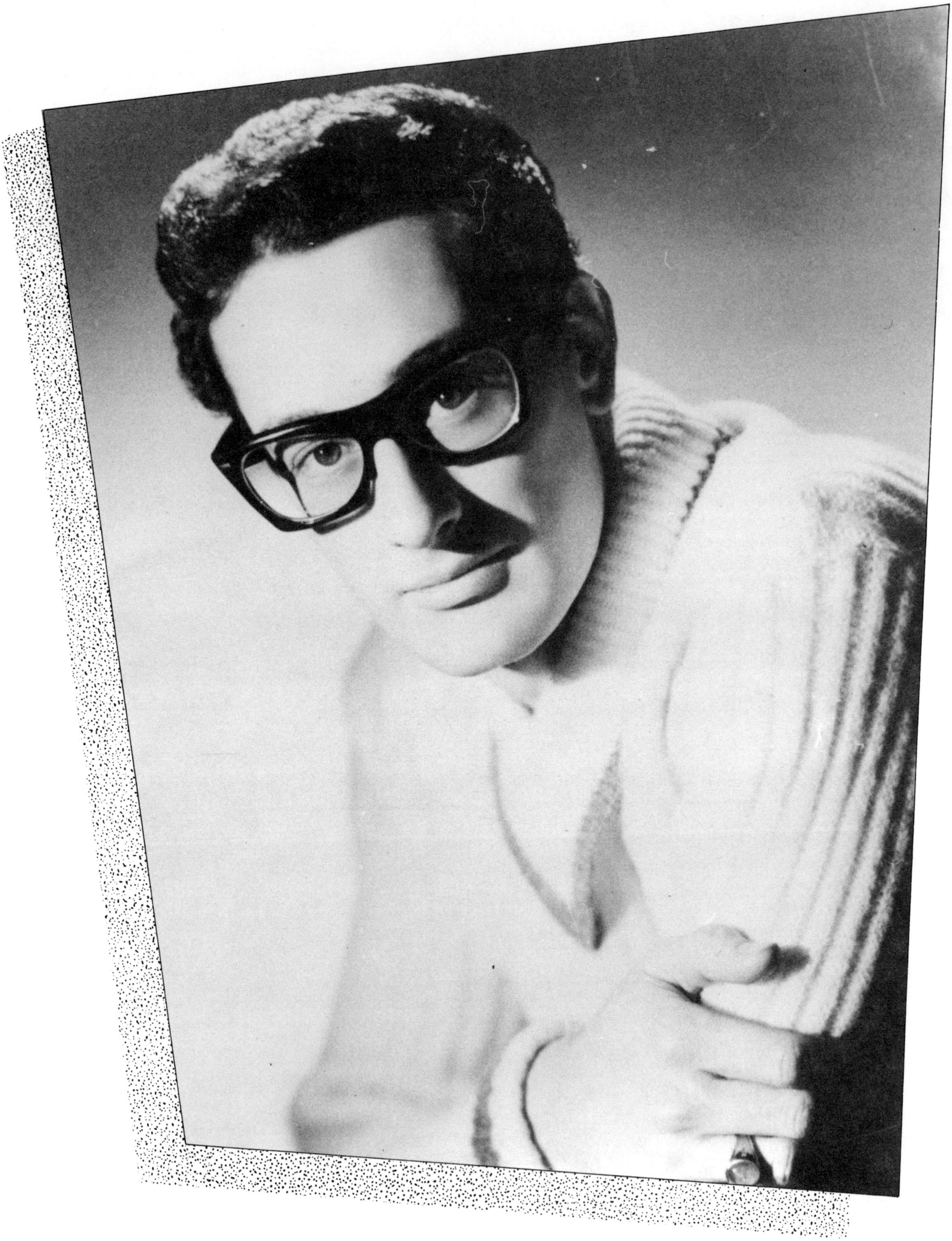

Song Stories

THAT'LL BE THE DAY

This was the first hit for Holly and the Crickets. It reached the number 3 position on Billboard's Top 100 in September 1957 and stayed in the Top 100 for three months! The title is based on a phrase from a 1956 John Wayne movie, *The Searchers*. Produced by Norman Petty at his studios in Clovis, New Mexico, February 1957. The record was released under the Crickets' name, since Holly's name was still tied up with his first record company, Decca (a parent company to his second record company Brunswick/Coral).

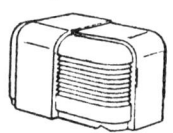

I'M LOOKING FOR SOMEONE TO LOVE

The flip side of *"That'll Be The Day"* written in a 12-bar blues pattern, but with a bright sound. John Goldrosen ("Buddy Holly — His Life and Music") states that the recording is an "excellent example of the Cricket's 'total sound.'" Holly plays combinations of R&B and country licks on his instrumental breaks, mixing them with rock into his unique rockabilly sound.

WORDS OF LOVE

Released by Holly in June 1957, but the first hit of this song was by the Diamonds whose version was released just prior to Holly's. This was Holly's first record to be "overdubbed," a process he then did quite often — singing and then playing lead guitar and laying on rhythm guitar. (He may be the first rock artist to use overdub.) Recorded in a faithful reproduction by the Beatles; released as in Ep in the U.K. *(BEATLES FOR SALE II)* and on the U.S. Lp, *BEATLES VI*.

PEGGY SUE

Holly's second single as a solo artist sold over 5 million units! Produced by Petty and released September 1957, it reached number 3 on Billboard's Top 100 at the end of December. The recording "showcased" Holly's hiccuping vocal style; the sound like a *catch* in his voice that was so effective in this song. In fact, this song embodies the "Holly" sound to most people. Originally called *"Cindy Lou,"* Holly agreed to change the title in honor of drummer Jerry Allison's girlfriend. Listen closely to the melding of Allison's drums and Holly's steady guitar rhythms on this recording...these were to become a strong influence on scores of rock and rollers to come!

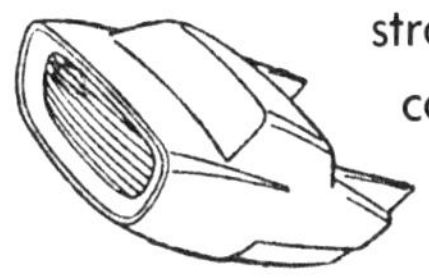

EVERYDAY

This "B" side contrast to *"Peggy Sue"* is sweet and quiet. It features Norman Petty on celeste (was this the forerunner to the famous Rhodes piano sound in ballads of the '70s?), and the only drumming being that of Jerry Allison slapping his knees.

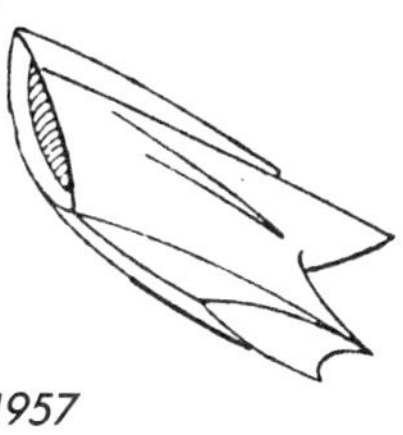

Marquee from the Crickets' first tour, August-September 1957

Rocking out at Alan Freed's "Holiday Show," Labor Day 1957
Niki Sullivan, Jerry Allison, Buddy Holly, Joe Mauldin

*Single cover from "**The Buddy Holly Boxed Set — The Portrait Series**" released in the U.K. by MCA Records LTD*

That'll Be The Day

Words and Music by NORMAN PETTY,
BUDDY HOLLY and JERRY ALLISON

Moderately, with a beat

Verse I

Well, you give me all your lov-in' and your tur-tle-dov-in', All your hugs an' kiss-es an' your mon-ey too;— Well, you know you love me, ba-by, Un-til you tell me, may-be, that some day, well, I'll be through!

© 1957 MPL COMMUNICATIONS, INC. and WREN MUSIC COMPANY
© Renewed 1985 MPL COMMUNICATIONS, INC. and WREN MUSIC COMPANY
International Copyright Secured   All Rights Reserved

Chorus

Well, THAT'LL BE THE DAY, when you say, good-bye, Yes, THAT'LL BE THE DAY, when you make me cry, Ah, you say you're gon-na leave, you know it's a lie, 'cause THAT'LL BE THE DAY when I die. Well, when I die.

Verse II

When Cu-pid shot his dart, He shot it at your heart, So if we ev-er part and I leave you, You say you told me an' you told me bold-ly, That some day, well, I'll be through. Well,

D.S. al Fine

I'M LOOKIN' FOR SOMEONE TO LOVE

Words and Music by BUDDY HOLLY
and NORMAN PETTY

1. Stay-in' at home, wait-in' for you, Just won't get it 'cause you say we're thru, An' I'm look-in' for some-one to love, I'm look-in' for some-one to love; Well, if you're not here, my ba-by,

2. Play-in' the field, all the day long, Since I found out that I was wronged, Now

3. Caught my-self think-in' of you, You can't love me and an-oth-er one too. Well,

© 1957 MPL COMMUNICATIONS, INC. and WREN MUSIC COMPANY
© Renewed 1985 MPL COMMUNICATIONS, INC. and WREN MUSIC COMPANY
International Copyright Secured   All Rights Reserved

I don't care,— Be-cause I'M LOOK-IN' FOR SOME-ONE TO LOVE.

4. Drunk __ man,__ Street __ car,__ Foot __ slipped... There you are,__ Now I'm LOOK-IN' FOR SOME-ONE TO LOVE, I'M LOOK-IN' FOR SOME-ONE TO LOVE;— Well, if you're not here,__my ba-by, I don't care,—Be-cause I'M LOOK-IN' FOR SOME-ONE TO LOVE.

WORDS OF LOVE

Words and Music by
BUDDY HOLLY

Very brightly

Hold me close and tell me how you feel,

Tell me love is real;

Oh, Oh;

© 1957 MPL COMMUNICATIONS, INC.
© Renewed 1985 MPL COMMUNICATIONS, INC.
International Copyright Secured   All Rights Reserved

Words Of Love you whisper soft and true, "Dar-ling, I love you;" Oh, _____ Oh. Oh. _____

PEGGY SUE

Words and Music by JERRY ALLISON,
NORMAN PETTY and BUDDY HOLLY

Very brightly

mf

If you knew ___ PEG-GY SUE, ___ Then you'd know why
PEG-GY SUE, ___ PEG-GY SUE, ___ Oh, how my heart

I feel blue ___ A-bout Peg-gy, ___ 'Bout my PEG-GY SUE; ___
yearns for you, ___ Oh, Pa-heg-gy, ___ My Pa-heg-gy Sue; ___

Oh, well, I love you, gal, ___ Yes, I love you, PEG-GY SUE:

© 1957 MPL COMMUNICATIONS, INC. and WREN MUSIC COMPANY
© Renewed 1985 MPL COMMUNICATIONS, INC. and WREN MUSIC COMPANY
International Copyright Secured   All Rights Reserved

PEG-GY SUE, ___ PEG-GY SUE, ___ Pret-ty, pret-ty, pret-ty, pret-ty, PEG-GY SUE, ___ Oh, my Peg-gy, ___ My PEG-GY SUE; ___ Oh, well, I love you gal, ___ and I need you, PEG-GY SUE. ___

I love you, PEG-GY SUE, With a love so rare and true, Oh, Peg-gy, My PEG-GY SUE;

Oh, well, I love you, gal, Yes, I want you, PEG-GY SUE.

D. S. al Fine

EVERYDAY

Words and Music by NORMAN PETTY
and CHARLES HARDIN

Very brightly

EV - 'RY DAY it's a-get-tin' clos-er, Go-ing fast-er than a roll-er-coast-er, Love like yours will tru-ly come my way.

Copyright © 1957 (Renewed) by Peer International Corporation
All Rights Reserved

EV - 'RY DAY it's a-gettin' fast-er, Ev-'ry-one said, "Go on up and ask her", Love like yours will tru-ly come my way.

EV - 'RY DAY seems a lit-tle long-er, Ev-'ry way love's a lit-tle strong-er, Come what may, do you ev-er long for true love from me? EV-'RY DAY it's a-get-tin' clos-er, Go-ing fast-er than a roll-er-coast-er; Love like yours will tru-ly come my way. way.

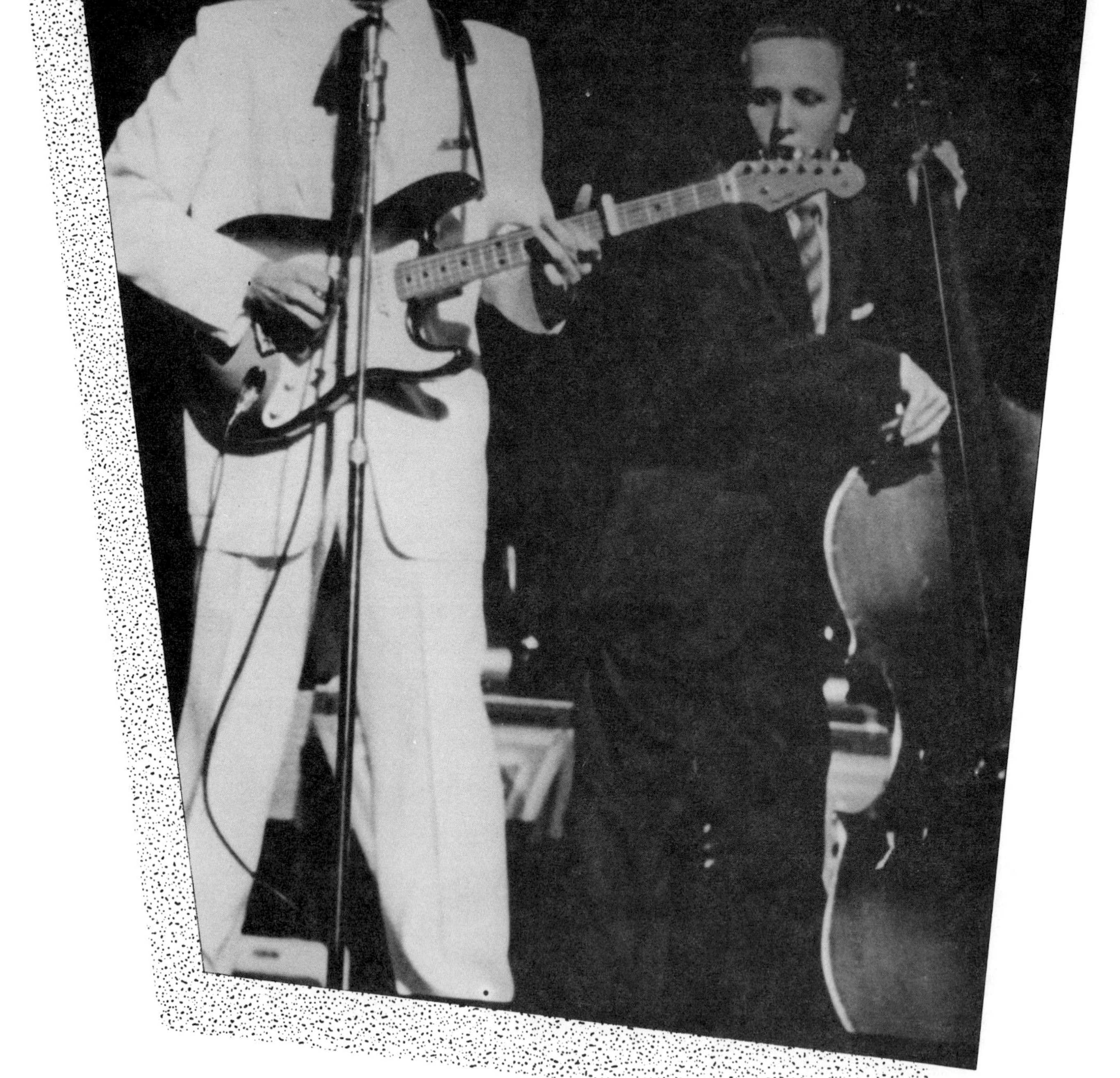

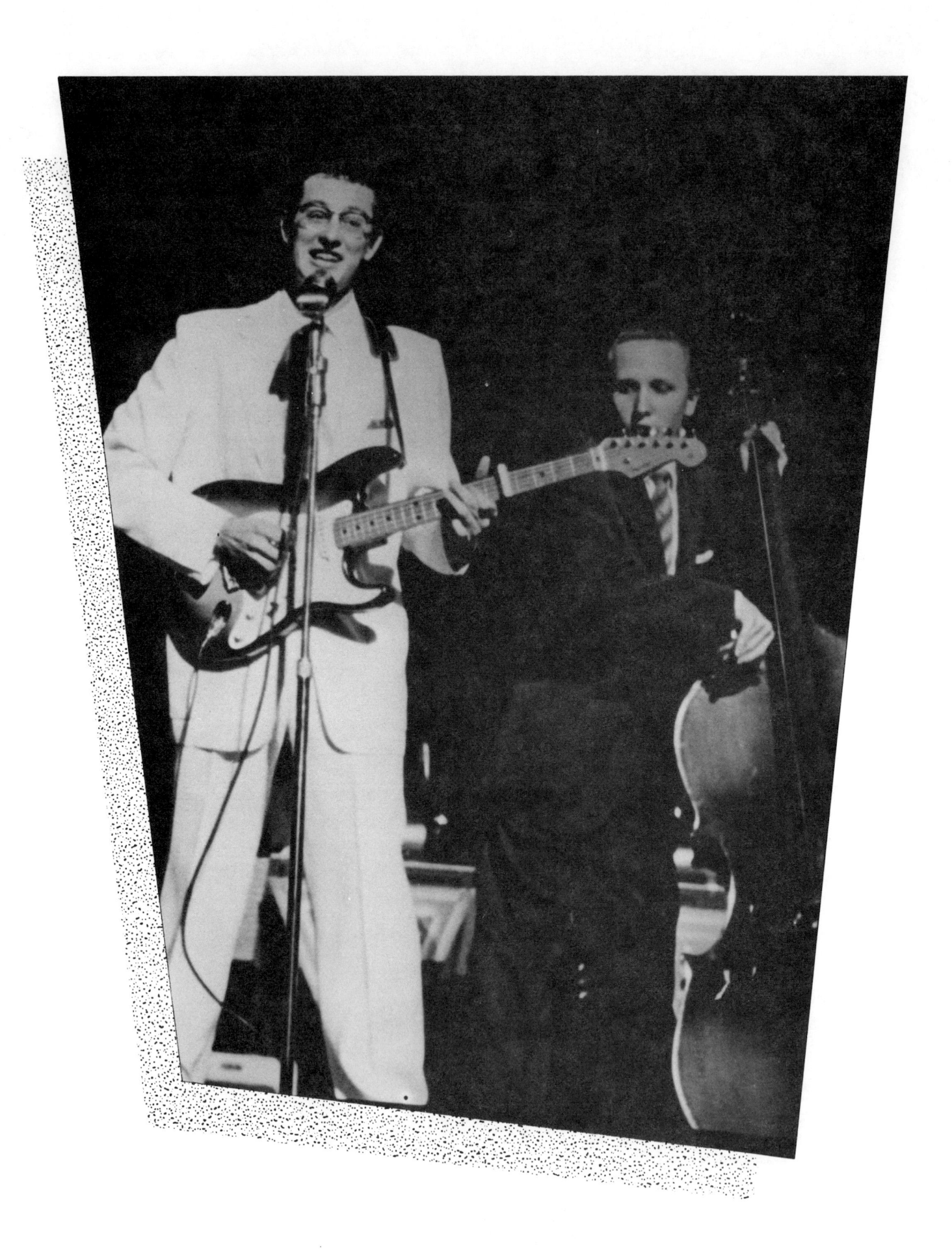

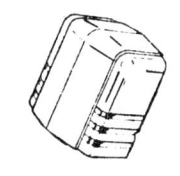

Song Stories

OH BOY!

The Crickets' second single released October, 1957; originally written as a country song by Sonny West and Bill Tilghman with additional lyric by Norman Petty. Holly heard the song in Petty's studio and arranged it in what turned out to be the best example of the Crickets' rockabilly style of playing. The song hit number 10 in Billboard early in '58 and sold over a million copies. It was also a number 1 hit for Mickey Most and Mud in the U.K. in 1975.

NOT FADE AWAY

"Oh Boy!'s" flip side had a Bo Diddley beat, and musically displayed Holly's great sense of control over the styles of the day, along with his abilities to create his own. This was the Rolling Stones first big hit and Bo Diddley recorded it himself in the '70s.

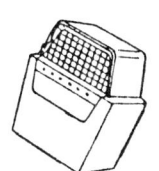

YOU'VE GOT LOVE/AN EMPTY CUP/ ROCK ME MY BABY/ LAST NIGHT

The first three songs were recorded for the Lp THE CHIRPING CRICKETS during a 5-day break from the Crickets' first tour in September '57. The break was a result of ordinances in several Southern cities that ludicrously prevented whites and blacks from performing together (the tour included Chuck Berry, Fats Domino, The Everly Brothers, Paul Anka, the Drifters and more!). With time short and the record company impatient for an album, Holly and the Crickets joined Norman Petty at Tinker Air Force Base, Oklahoma, where Petty was playing a gig. They set up equipment in the Officer's club and overnight recorded the tunes. Petty then took the tapes back to his studio for overdubbing (many critics feel that this detracted from the strength of the Crickets' sound and it would have been better if Holly had been in on the "sweetening"). The guitar solo on "Rock Me My Baby" is touted as being Holly's best and the Crickets' instrumental talents on this cut are lauded as well. "Last Night," cut in an earlier May '57 session is a straight-ahead rock and roll ballad. THE CHIRPING CRICKETS album was released by Brunswick in November 1957.

Early fall 1957 on the "Show Of Stars" Tour

December 1957, getting ready to perform on the Ed Sullivan Show

Marquee from the New York Paramount Christmas Shows, 1957

*Single cover from "**The Buddy Holly Boxed Set — The Portrait Series**" released in the U.K. by MCA Records LTD*

Buddy, Jerry, Joe performing, Alan Freed's Christmas Show

OH BOY!

*Words and Music by SUNNY WEST,
BILL TILGHMAN and NORMAN PETTY*

Bright tempo

All of my love, all of my kiss-in', You don't know what you been miss-in', Oh Boy! (Oh Boy!) When you're with me, Oh Boy! (Oh Boy!) The world can see that you were meant for me.

© 1957 WREN MUSIC COMPANY
© Renewed 1985 WREN MUSIC COMPANY
International Copyright Secured   All Rights Reserved

D7
G
All of my life I been wait - in', To - night there'll be no
G
C
G
hes - i - tat - in', Oh Boy! (Oh Boy!) When you're with me, Oh Boy! (Oh Boy!) The
G
C♯dim
D7
G
C
G
world can see that you were meant for me.
D7
G
Stars ap - pear and shad - ows fall - in', You can hear my heart call - in', A

lit-tle bit o' lov-in' makes ev-'ry-thing right, An' I'm gon-na see my ba-by to-ni-ight! All o' my love, all o' my kiss-in', You don't know what you been miss-in', Oh Boy! (Oh Boy!) When you're with me, Oh Boy! (Oh Boy!) The world can see that you were meant for

41

NOT FADE AWAY

Words and Music by CHARLES HARDIN
and NORMAN PETTY

Brightly

1. I'm gon-na tell you how it's gon-na be,
2. My love is big-ger than a Cad-il-lac,
3. I'm gon-na tell you how it's gon-na be,

You're gon-na give-a your love to me.
I try to show it and you drive me back.
You're gon-na give-a your love to me.

I wan-na love you night and day;
Your love for me has got to be real;
love to last more than one day;

© 1957 MPL COMMUNICATIONS, INC. and WREN MUSIC COMPANY
© Renewed 1985 MPL COMMUNICATIONS, INC. and WREN MUSIC COMPANY
International Copyright Secured   All Rights Reserved

Ab
Bb7
Eb
Ab
You know my love _ NOT_ FADE A- WAY. ____
For you to know_ just_ how I feel. ____
A love that's love _ NOT_ FADE A- WAY. ____
mf
f
Eb
Bb7
Eb
Well, you know my love _ NOT_ FADE A- WAY. ____
A love for real _ NOT_ FADE A- WAY. ____
A love that's love _ NOT_ FADE A- WAY. ____
mf
1.
Eb
Ab
Eb
Repeat, then to
2.
Eb
Ab
Eb
Repeat, then to
mf
Repeat, then D. S.
Repeat, then D. S. al Fine
Fine
Repeat several times gradually softer
Eb
Ab
Eb
Eb
Ab
Eb
pp
ppp

YOU'VE GOT LOVE

Words and Music by JOHNNY WILSON
ROY ORBISON and NORMAN PETTY

Moderately, with a beat

You've got two lips that look so fine,— You've got one_ heart I wish was mine;— Love, real_ love You've Got Love! You've got

© 1957 WREN MUSIC COMPANY
© Renewed 1985 WREN MUSIC COMPANY
International Copyright Secured   All Rights Reserved

two arms that you could use, To make me lose my blues, Love, sweet love, You've got Love! You've got love, real love, You've got love, sweet love,

A7
D7
You've Got Love, that is true, I want
You've got me, in a spin, I love the
G
D7
on - ly you; You've got two eyes so you can see,
spin I'm in; You've got two hands I love to touch You've got
G
D7
C
D7
Your love was made for me;
good love I need so much;
Love! true love, You've Got
1.
G
C9
Cm6
G
Fm6
D7
2.
G
C
F♯6
G6
Love! You've got Love!
f

AN EMPTY CUP
(And A Broken Date)

Words and Music by ROY ORBISON
and NORMAN PETTY

Slowly

Chorus:

One lonely night, at this drive-in,

And now I know what a fool I've been,

She was to meet me, we had a date,

A date at sev-en, I dreamed of heav-en, Now it's way past eight; She just drove by with an-oth-er guy, No won-der I can't help but cry. To think she nev-er cared just tears me

Eb
F7
up; Now all I have to show for love
Bb7
Tacet
Eb
Ab
Is An Emp - ty Cup Just like the snow, my love is
Eb
Ab
Eb
Ab
gone, I've hit the bot-tom, now I'm a -
1. Eb
Ab
Eb
Bb7
2. Eb
Ab
Eb
lone. One lone - ly lone.

ROCK ME MY BABY

Words and Music by SUSAN HEATHER
and SHORTY LONG

Moderate Rock

Verse:
1. Oh, well-a, Put your arms around me now, And try your best to squeeze me; Love me, baby you know how, Yes, ROCK ME, MY BABY.

Chorus:
Well, I'm rock-in' like a hick-o-ry-dick-o-ry-dock,

© 1957 WREN MUSIC COMPANY
© Renewed 1985 WREN MUSIC COMPANY
International Copyright Secured   All Rights Reserved

Rock-a-bye, my ba-by; Up and down and 'round the clock, Well, ROCK ME, MY BA-BY. BA-BY.

Verse:
2. Plant your kiss - es on my lips. And make me bub - ble o - ver;
3. Tell me that you love me too And say you'll nev - er leave me;

Thrill me to my fin - ger tips, Well, ROCK ME, MY BA-BY. Well, I'm
No one loves you like I do, Well, ROCK ME, MY BA-BY. Well, I'm

LAST NIGHT

Words and Music by JOE MAULDIN
and NORMAN PETTY

Slowly, with strong beat

LAST NIGHT as I watched the stars from my win-dow, I prayed Lord a-bove to guide and pro-tect you, Tho' I'm not want-ed now, I still love you some-how, That is my on-ly prayer for

© 1957 WREN MUSIC COMPANY
© Renewed 1985 WREN MUSIC COMPANY
International Copyright Secured   All Rights Reserved

you. LAST NIGHT, as I gazed thru the mist in my eyes, I wanted you, dear, to hold you so near, But silence tells me, You didn't hear my plea. I missed you so much since you

53

left me, My heart ached a-part since you left me; Though I'm not want-ed now, I still love you some-how; That is my on-ly prayer, for you. LAST you.

Late 1957, Canada (unidentified man)

Publicity pic, January '58

Single cover from "**The Buddy Holly Boxed Set — The Portrait Series**" released in the U.K. by MCA Records LTD

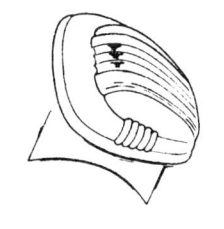

Song Stories

I'M GONNA LOVE YOU TOO/LISTEN TO ME

Released by Holly in February 1958. It was during the recording session for this record, Spring '57, that a cricket was heard in the echo chamber of Petty's studio. The chirping constantly interrupted the session, but searches found nothing. In one of the takes, the cricket behaved and chirped in tempo at the very end of the song. The chirps were retained as a gimmick, hence the group's name and the title of the first album. The U.S. release of this single was not well-timed by the record company, since two tunes were still on the charts, therefore, although these are considered some of Holly's finest recordings, they were not commercial successes. "Listen To Me" is especially highlighted by the overdubbing effects and changes in vocal dynamics, plus Holly's guitar. "I'm Gonna Love You Too" is "punctuated" with Holly's colorful emphasis on various words.

MAYBE BABY

Written early in the Crickets' career, but recorded at the Tinker Air Force Base session, September 1957. Released in the U.K. to benefit from the Crickets' tour there in March '58 (the tour increased sales to the point where they had 4 singles —"Oh Boy!," "Peggy Sue," "Maybe Baby" and "Listen To Me" — on the top 30 chart in a single week). Released in the U.S. in February '58, it reached 18 on Billboard's Top 100 by the end of March. Ella Holley, Buddy's mother, provided several lines and inspiration for this song, but wasn't credited until much later (probably because it wasn't cool for a rock star's mom to co-write his songs). Jerry Allison's drum beat, influenced by Little Richard's "Lucille," is noted as a strongly complementary element in the tight arrangement of the song.

LOOK AT ME

A cut from the Lp "Buddy Holly" released March 1958 as Holly's first solo album included the singles "Peggy Sue/Everyday," "I'm Gonna Love You Too/Listen To Me," "Rave On" plus three songs recorded by other rock greats (Presley, Fats Domino, Little Richard).

"Maybe Baby" sheet music cover

MAYBE BABY

Words and Music by NORMAN PETTY
and CHARLES HARDIN

Moderato with a steady beat

dim. poco a poco   *p*

MAY-BE, BA-BY, I'll have you,___ MAY-BE, BA-BY, You'll be true,___

MAY-BE, BA-BY, I'll have you___ for me.___

It's fun-ny, hon-ey, you don't care,___ You nev-er lis-ten to my prayer,___

© 1957 MPL COMMUNICATIONS, INC. and WREN MUSIC COMPANY
© Renewed 1985 MPL COMMUNICATIONS, INC. and WREN MUSIC COMPANY
International Copyright Secured   All Rights Reserved

MAY-BE, BA-BY, you will love me some-day. Well, you are the one that makes me sad, And you are the one that makes me glad, when some-day you want me, I'll be there, wait and see. Oh, MAY-BE, BA-BY, I'll have you, MAY-BE, BA-BY, you'll be true, MAY-BE, BA-BY, I'll have you for me. me.

I'M GONNA LOVE YOU TOO

Words and Music by JOE MAULDIN,
NIKI SULLIVAN and NORMAN PETTY

Moderato - With a solid rock

1. You're gon-na say you'll-a miss me, You're gon-na say you'll-a kiss me,
2. It's gon-na hap-pen some-day, You're gon-na see things my way,

© 1957, 1958 MPL COMMUNICATIONS, INC. and WREN MUSIC COMPANY
© Renewed 1985, 1986 MPL COMMUNICATIONS, INC. and WREN MUSIC COMPANY
International Copyright Secured   All Rights Reserved

You're gon-na say you'll-a love me, 'cause I'm-a gon-na love you too. I
don't care what you told me, You're gon-na say you'll a - hold me,
You're gon-na tell me sweet things, You're gon-na make-a my heart sing,
You're gon-na say you'll-a love me, 'cause I'm a-gon-na love you too.
You're gon-na hear those-a bells ring, 'cause I'm a-gon-na love you too.

Aft-er all, an-oth-er fel-la took ya, But I still can't o-ver-look ya,

I'm a-gon-na do my best to hook ya, After all is said and done.

You're gon-na say you'll-a miss me, You're gon-na say you'll-a kiss me,

You're gon-na say you'll-a love me, 'cause I'm a-gon-na love you too.

1.
Ah, Ah,

63

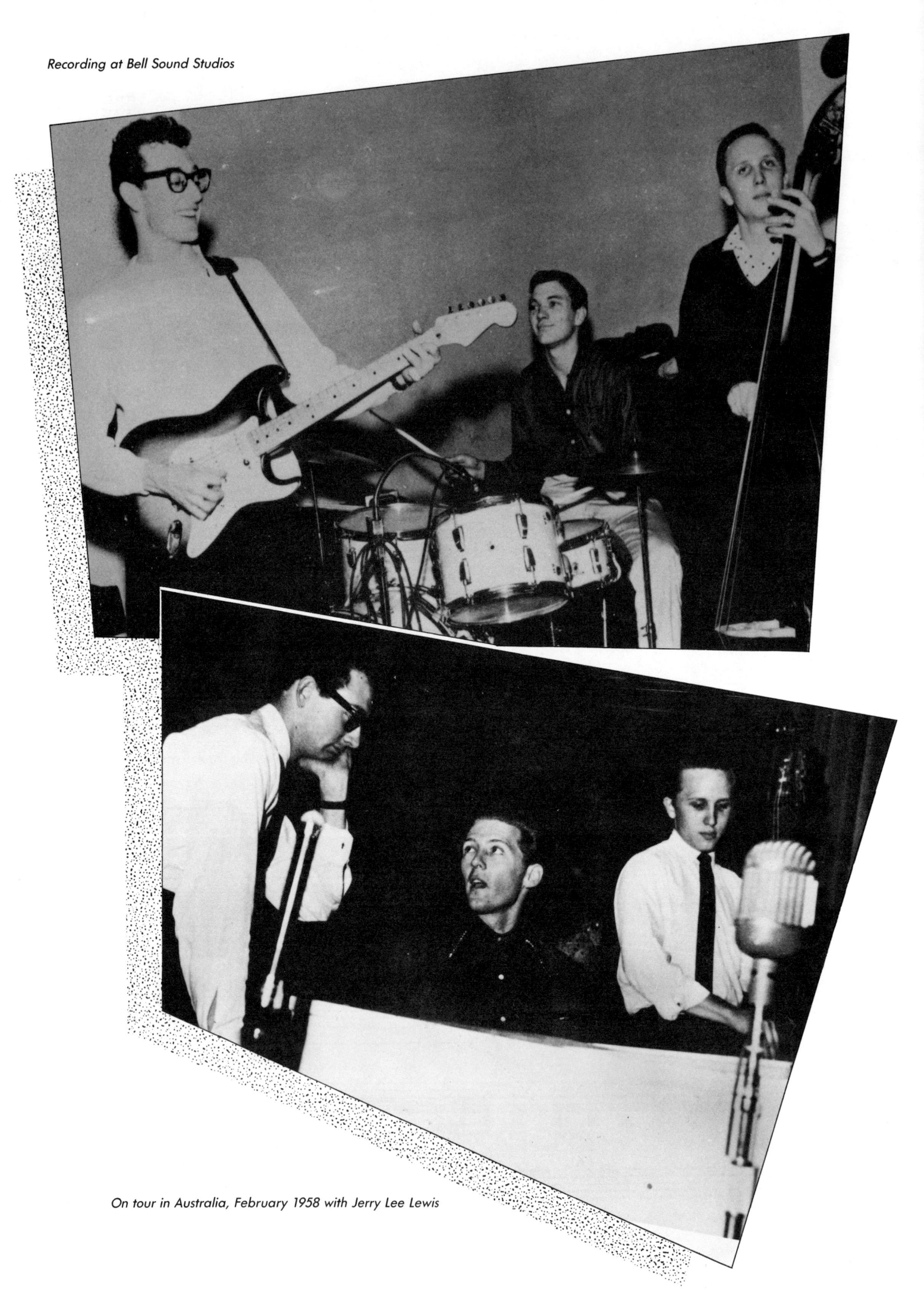

Recording at Bell Sound Studios

On tour in Australia, February 1958 with Jerry Lee Lewis

LISTEN TO ME

Words and Music by CHARLES HARDIN
and NORMAN PETTY

Moderato, not too slowly, with a Rockin' beat

Lis-ten To me, _____ and hold me tight, _____
and you will see _____ our love go right, _____
My on-ly dar-ling, lis-ten close-ly to

© 1957, 1958 MPL COMMUNICATIONS, INC. and WREN MUSIC COMPANY
© Renewed 1985, 1986 MPL COMMUNICATIONS, INC. and WREN MUSIC COMPANY
International Copyright Secured   All Rights Reserved

me.

Your eyes will see _____ what love can know now

how sweet sweet-hearts can be. _____ Lis-ten To

Me. _____ hear what I say, _____ Our hearts can

Bb C7 F Gm F
be near - er each day, My on - ly
Bb C7 Gm7 C7
1. F Gm F
dar - ling, lis - ten close - ly to me.
Bb C7
2. F Gm F Bb F
me.

LOOK AT ME

Words and Music by NORMAN PETTY,
BUDDY HOLLY and JERRY ALLISON

Hey, hey, Look At Me and tell me, What's gonna happen to you;

When you've broken too many people's hearts, And

can't find anyone new Say, say, look at me an'

© 1958, 1959 MPL COMMUNICATIONS, INC. and WREN MUSIC COMPANY
© Renewed 1986, 1987 MPL COMMUNICATIONS, INC. and WREN MUSIC COMPANY
International Copyright Secured   All Rights Reserved

tell me, _____ 'Bout ___ that twinkle in your eye, Is that twinkle in your eye meant for me, Or meant for some other guy? _____ Look At Me from now on, _____ Know the love _____ we share; _____ Look at me from _____ now on, _____

Let me know_ you care;_

Hey, hey, Look At Me an' tell me,_ What's_ gon-na hap-pen to you;_

When you've spo-ken sweet words_ of love to me, And

I want to mar-ry you._ you.

70

Song Stories

RAVE ON

A rock anthem released late April 1958; some people consider it "perfect" and others "one of the most exciting that Holly and the Crickets ever made." It made it only to #38 in Billboard, but it was the Crickets' biggest hit in the U.K., making #5 on the charts by early summer. Penned by "Oh Boy!" writers, West and Tilghman, it's one of the most "fun" tunes, highlighting the "hiccuping," multisyllable style of Holly. Remember "We-ell-ell-ell-ell-ell"? On the down side, one very straight radio station termed it "mood music for stealing hubcaps."

TAKE YOUR TIME

Interestingly this tune uses the same chord pattern as "Look At Me" from the same album. This flip side of "Rave On" has a peculiar instrumental mixture with Holly on acoustic guitar, Norman Petty on organ and a mixed backing of effects by Allison.

FOOL'S PARADISE

Released May 1958, the flip side of "Think It Over" this hit 58 on Billboards Hot 100 and is known for its fine musical arrangement.

IT'S SO EASY/LONESOME TEARS

Released in September 1958, "It's So Easy" was the last Crickets' recording to feature Holly as lead singer. It didn't show on the U.S. charts, but had some popularity in the U.K. This was also guitarist Tommy Allsup's debut with the Crickets in performance. Listen for his country style on the recording that sounds remarkably steel guitarish, and blends well with the rest of the Crickets, as well as with Holly's playing. The structure of this song is said to have some impact on various other composer's writing, including the Beatles. Linda Ronstadt had a big hit with this tune in the '70s.

Rehearsing at the Trocadero Theatre at London's Elephant and Castle, March 1958

Getting ready to tour the U.K., March 1958

Single cover from "**The Buddy Holly Boxed Set — The Portrait Series**" released in the U.K. by MCA Records LTD

Performing on BBC TV's "Off The Record," March 27, 1958

RAVE ON

Words and Music by SUNNY WEST,
BILL TILGHMAN and NORMAN PETTY

The lit-tle things you say and do, They make me want to be with you-hoo-hoo, RAVE ON! It's a cra-zy feel-in' and
(The) way you dance and hold me tight, The way you kiss and say good-ni- hi-hight,

I know it's got me reel-in' When you say, "I love you," RAVE

1. ON. Well, the
2. ON.

© 1957, 1958 WREN MUSIC COMPANY
© Renewed 1985, 1986 WREN MUSIC COMPANY
International Copyright Secured   All Rights Reserved

Chorus
F7 Bb7 F
Well - ell - ell, RAVE ON ! It's a cra - zy feel - in' and I know it's —
F C7 C11 F C7
got me reel - in', I'm' so glad that you're re-veal - in' your love for
F F7 Bb7 F
me! RAVE ON, RAVE ON and tell _ me, Tell me not_
F Bb F C7
— to be lone - ly, Tell me you love me on - ly,
1. F Bb F F7
RAVE ON to me. Well - ell - ell
2. F Bb F
RAVE ON to me.

TAKE YOUR TIME

Words and Music by NORMAN PETTY
and BUDDY HOLLY

Moderato

TAKE YOUR TIME,— I can wait,— For all the love— I know will be mine if— you TAKE YOUR TIME.

TAKE YOUR TIME— though it's late,— Heart strings will sing like a string of twine— if— you TAKE YOUR TIME.—

© 1958 MPL COMMUNICATIONS, INC. and WREN MUSIC COMPANY
© Renewed 1986 MPL COMMUNICATIONS, INC. and WREN MUSIC COMPANY
International Copyright Secured   All Rights Reserved

F F7 Bb F C7
TAKE YOUR TIME and take mine too, I have time to
mf mp
F F7 Bb F G7
spend. TAKE YOUR TIME go with me through times 'til all times
mf
C7 F Bb C7 F Bb
end. TAKE YOUR TIME, I can wait,
mp
C7 F C7 F C7
For all the love I know will be mine if
F C7 1. F Gm7 C9 2. F oC11 F oC11 F
you TAKE YOUR TIME. TIME.
dim. poco a poco
rall.
pp

FOOL'S PARADISE

Words and Music by SONNY LE GLAIRE,
HORACE LINSLEY and NORMAN PETTY

Moderato

You took me up to heav-en, when you took me in your arms, I was daz-zled by your kiss-es, blind-ed by your charms, I was lost, in a FOOL'S PAR-A-DISE;

© 1958 WREN MUSIC COMPANY
© Renewed 1986 WREN MUSIC COMPANY
International Copyright Secured   All Rights Reserved

Good and lost, in a FOOL'S PAR-A-DISE!
When you told me that you loved me, I gave my heart to you. And I wondered if there could be an-y truth in love so new, I was lost, in a FOOL'S PAR-A-DISE;

Good and lost, in a FOOL'S PAR-A-DISE! The whole world was my king-dom, and your love, the gem in my crown; Then I saw you glance at a new ro-mance, and my love came tum-bling down! Though you treat me kind-a cool-ish, and may

F C7 F7 B♭ F7 B♭
never let me know, that you think I'm be - ing fool - ish, be -
B♭ F7 B♭ Bdim C7 Cdim C7
cause I love you so, I'll still get lost, in a FOOL'S PAR - A-
mf
F Bdim C7 Cdim C7
DISE; Lost with you, in a FOOL'S PAR - A -
mf
1. F Gm7 C7
DISE! You
2. F E♭9 Fmaj7
DISE!
ff

IT'S SO EASY

Words and Music by BUDDY HOLLY
and NORMAN PETTY

Moderately bright (good beat)

IT'S SO EAS-Y to fall in love,_ IT'S SO EAS-Y to_ fall_ in love._

Verse I
Peo-ple tell me love's for fools,_ So here I go_ break-ing all of the rules._

CHORUS
It seems so eas-y, (Hum),____ so dog-gone eas-y;

© 1958 MPL COMMUNICATIONS, INC. and WREN MUSIC COMPANY
© Renewed 1986 MPL COMMUNICATIONS, INC. and WREN MUSIC COMPANY
International Copyright Secured   All Rights Reserved

Bb
Bb7
Eb
C7
(Hum). It seems so eas-y, Where you're con - cerned my
F7
Bb
F9
Eb
F7
heart has learned; IT'S SO EAS - Y to fall in love,
mf
Bb
Eb
1. F7
Bb
F7
Bb
Fine
IT'S SO EAS - Y to fall in love!
fall in love!
Verse II
Bb
F9
Eb
F7
Bb
Eb
F7
Bb
Bb7
To Chorus
Look in - to your heart and see
What your love book has set a - part for me. It seems so
3
f
D.S. 𝄋 al Fine

LONESOME TEARS

Words and Music by
BUDDY HOLLY

Moderato and steadily

Lone - some Tears sad and blue, I shed Lone - some Tears for you, Guess you know I know why I cried when you said good-bye. (I cried for you

© 1958 MPL COMMUNICATIONS, INC.
© Renewed 1986 MPL COMMUNICATIONS, INC.
International Copyright Secured   All Rights Reserved

Lone-some Tears) When you left and you said, "I'm gone", Lone-some Tears fell all night long. Yes, you know I know I cried when you said good-bye. You left me here all a-lone. Hear me call-in', won't you come back home. Love me like you

F7
Bb7
did be - fore,
Now need I tell you more?
mf
mp
Eb
Cm
G+
Lone - some Tears,
Sad and blue,
I shed Lone - some
Ab
Eb
C+
F7
Bb7
Tears for you,
Guess you know I know I cried when you said good -
1.
Eb
Adim
Abm
4 fr.
Eb
Bb7
bye.
(I cried for you Lone - some Tears.)
2.
Eb
Adim
Abm
4 fr.
Eb
Ab
Eb
bye.
(Those Lone - some Tears.)
rall.
p

Song Stories

HEARTBEAT/WELL ALL RIGHT

"*Heartbeat*" was released as a Buddy Holly solo, and was co-written by Holly's earliest partner, Bob Montgomery, and Norman Petty. Listen to the record and note the alternating vocal and instrumental lines. Although this was not a big hit, it does show Holly's innate sense of "pop" in the fact that hard-driving rock was petering out at this point in '58 as MOR and folk music were resurging. Consequently, this does not have the driving beat of his previous arrangements, it does have the then current "chalypso" beat. "*Well All Right*" was based on a phrase used by Little Richard, and is also more in keeping with the chart hits of the time with an acoustic sound, almost folk-like. The lyric is timeless, the painful cry of youth...the misunderstood in love. This tune was recorded by several artists, most notably Blind Faith.

PEGGY SUE GOT MARRIED

One of six songs Holly recorded on a tape recorder in his New York City apartment that were released after his death. As a true September child, Holly was known to polish and rewrite these tunes until he did a final tape in January '59. "*Peggy Sue*" had become a legend to the point where it was even mentioned in several other rock songs. Since the real event of Peggy Sue's marriage to Crickets' drummer Jerry Allison had occurred, Holly decided to continue the story, as his father suggested, in a sequel. The music is somewhat redolent of "*Peggy Sue*" using the same chord progressions, however some of the sound is obscured by the "sweetening" and overdubbing added by the record company to the tapes. This was taped the evening before Holly left on what was to be his final tour, and released posthumously July 1959.

TRUE LOVE WAYS/MOONDREAMS

In light of the times, and pressure from his record company, Holly agreed to do some ballads in the fall of '58. "*True Love Ways*" was the best of a session held at the Pythian Temple in New York City. It was his first use of strings — a concept that as a rock and roller he had rejected several times. Released in 1960, Holly's version hit the mid-portion of the charts and Peter and Gordon's version hit the top 10 in 1965. "*Moondreams*" has a lush, pop sound.

LOVE'S MADE A FOOL OF YOU

Written in the summer of '58 with old friend Bob Montgomery, Holly hoped to have the Everly Bros. record it. Recorded as a demo at Petty's studio with a group of top studio musicians, it's notable for its Latin rhythmic influences and lead guitar sound (Tommy Allsup) with alternating vocal and instrumental lines. The Everlys had ties with other songwriters and did not record this; it was released posthumously in 1964 and recorded by several other artists, notably Tom Rush.

WHAT TO DO

Recorded on the New York City "home" tapes, Norman Petty added some really satisfactory sweetening, and it was released March '65 as a single (also released in a March 1960 Lp with some rather poor sweetening). A ballad, this lyric once more touches so closely on the young person's bittersweet experiences with a love that's been lost...reliving all the happenings and places that had been shared.

August 15, 1958, marriage to Maria Elena Santiago in Lubbock

Honeymooning in Acapulco with Jerry Allison and his fabled Peggy Sue

The last tour: D.J. Jim Lounsbury, The Big Bopper, Debbie Stevens, Frankie Sardo, Buddy

Waylon Jennings and Buddy on the last tour, January 1959

WELL ALL RIGHT

Words and Music by NORMAN PETTY, BUDDY HOLLY,
JERRY ALLISON and JOE MAULDIN

Moderato, with a strong beat

VERSE

WELL ALL RIGHT — so I'm — be-ing fool-ish, Well all right —
(WELL ALL RIGHT) — so I'm — go-in' stead-y, It's all right —

— let peo-ple know — A-bout the dreams and wish-es you —
— when peo-ple say, — That those — fool-ish kids can't be read-

— wish in the night — when lights are low. —
-y for the love — that comes their way. —

© 1958 MPL COMMUNICATIONS, INC. and WREN MUSIC COMPANY
© Renewed 1986 MPL COMMUNICATIONS, INC. and WREN MUSIC COMPANY
International Copyright Secured   All Rights Reserved

CHORUS

WELL ALL RIGHT,— WELL ALL RIGHT,— Oh, we'll live and love with all our might,— Well all right,— WELL ALL RIGHT,— Our life-time love will be all right,— WELL ALL RIGHT be all right.—

HEARTBEAT

Words and Music by BOB MONTGOMERY
and NORMAN PETTY

Moderato

Heart - beat, _____ why do you miss when my ba - by kiss - es me?
Heart - beat, _____ why do you skip when my ba - by's lips meet mine?

© 1958 WREN MUSIC COMPANY
© Renewed 1982 WREN MUSIC COMPANY
International Copyright Secured   All Rights Reserved

Heart - beat, _____ why does a love kiss __ stay
Heart - beat, _____ why do you flip, then __ give

in my mem - o - ry?
me a skip - beat sign?

Rid - dle - dee - pat, __ I know that new __ love
Rid - dle - dee - pat, __ and sing to me __ love's

thrills me, __ I know that true __ love
sto - ry, __ And bring to me __ love's

C G D7 G
will be. Heart - beat,
glo - ry. Heart - beat,
mp
C D7 C D7
why do you miss when my ba - by kiss - es
why do you miss when my ba - by kiss - es
G C G D7
me?
me?
1.
G C G D7
2.
G C G D7 G C G D7 GaddA
mf
dim. poco a poco
p

February 3, 1959

PEGGY SUE GOT MARRIED

Words and Music by
BUDDY HOLLY

Moderately, strong beat

Please don't tell,_ no, no, no;_ Don't say that I told_ you_ so;_
I just heard a rum-or from a friend._
I don't say_ that it's true,_ I'll just leave that up_ to_ you,_
If you don't_ be-lieve,_ I'll un-der-sta-ha-hand.(Un-der - sta - ha - hand).

Copyright © 1959 by Peer International Corporation
All Rights Reserved

You re-call the girl that's been in near-ly ev-'ry song; This is what I heard, of course the sto-ry could be wrong; She's the one, I've been told, That she's wear-in' a band of gold; PEG-GY SUE GOT MAR-RIED not long a-go.

PEG-GY SUE GOT MAR-RIED not long a-go.

MOONDREAMS

Words and Music by
NORMAN PETTY

Moderately

1. Strange things take place in my MOONDREAMS, As the lonely and loveless hours go by; Your face takes its place in ev'ry moonbeam,

2. Ah — — — — — — Ah — — — — — — Ah —

© 1957 WREN MUSIC COMPANY
© Renewed 1985 WREN MUSIC COMPANY
International Copyright Secured   All Rights Reserved

MOON-DREAMS bring thoughts gentle as a sigh;
Ah — — — — — — — — —
— — — MOON-DREAMS can be a sensation;
— MOON-DREAMS may be fascination;
Love can be our destination; You and

I can share this dream. ___ Wishing for you in my MOON-DREAMS ___ As the lonely and loveless hours go by, ___ Will do until you can share all my dreams, MOON-DREAMS, brought by moon-beams in the sky.

Late 1958 publicity still

TRUE LOVE WAYS

Words and Music by NORMAN PETTY
and BUDDY HOLLY

Slowly

Just you know why, why you and I will by and by know TRUE LOVE WAYS; Some-times we'll sigh, some-times we'll cry, And we'll know why, just you and I know TRUE LOVE

© 1958, 1960 MPL Communications, INC. and WREN MUSIC COMPANY
© Renewed 1986, 1988 MPL COMMUNICATIONS, INC. and WREN MUSIC COMPANY
International Copyright Secured   All Rights Reserved

WAYS. Through-out the days, our TRUE LOVE WAYS will bring us joys to share with those who real-ly care. Some-times we'll sigh, some-times we'll cry, And we'll know why, just you and I, know TRUE LOVE WAYS. Just you know I, know TRUE LOVE WAYS.

LOVE'S MADE A FOOL OF YOU

Words and Music by BUDDY HOLLY
and BOB MONTGOMERY

Moderately with a strong beat

You know love makes a fool of you,— You do an-y-thing— it- a
You know love makes fools of men,— But you don't care, you're gon-na

wants you to!— Love can make— you feel so good,— You
try a-gain!— Time goes by— it's a-pass-ing fast,— You

When it goes— like you think it should! Or it can make— you
think true love- a has come at last!— Bye and— bye— you're

© 1958, 1959 MPL COMMUNICATIONS, INC. and WREN MUSIC COMPANY
© Renewed 1986 MPL COMMUNICATIONS, INC. and WREN MUSIC COMPANY
International Copyright Secured   All Rights Reserved

cry at night,— When your ba-by don't treat you right;—
gon-na find,— Craz-y love-a has-a made you blind;—

When you're feel-in' sad and blue,— You know LOVE'S-A MADE A

1. FOOL OF YOU!—

2. FOOL OF YOU!— You know LOVE'S-A MADE A FOOL OF YOU!

WHAT TO DO

Words and Music by
BUDDY HOLLY

What to do, now that she doesn't want me, That's what haunts me, What to do What to do to keep from being lonely, Want her only,

Eb F7 Bb Eb Bb D7
What to do.
The re-cord hops
D7 Eb F A7 A7+ A7
and all the hap-py times we had,
The so-da shop,
A7 Bb C7 F7 Bb
The walks to school now makes me sad,
Oh,
What to do
I
Bb F7 Bb Eb F7 Bb
know my heart-ache's show-in',
Still not know-in',
Eb F7
1. Bb Eb F7
What to do.
2. Bb Eb6 Bb

DISCOGRAPHY

SINGLES

D = Decca; Br = Brunswick;
C = Coral; MCA = MCA

Record No.	Title	Date Released	Highest chart Position in Billboard Top 100
D 29854	Blue Days, Black Nights; Love Me	4/16/56	
D 30166	Modern Don Juan; You Are My One Desire	12/24/56	
Br 55009	That'll Be The Day; I'm Lookin' For Someone To Love	5/27/57	3
C 61852	Words Of Love; Mailman, Bring Me No More Blues	6/20/57	
D 30434	Rock Around With Ollie Vee; That'll Be The Day	9/2/57	
C 61885	Peggy Sue; Everyday	9/20/57	3
Br 55035	Oh Boy!; Not Fade Away	10/27/57	10
D 30543	Love Me; You Are My One Desire	1/6/58	
C 61947	I'm Gonna Love You Too; Listen To Me	2/5/58	
Br 55053	Maybe Baby; Tell Me How	2/12/58	18
C 61985	Rave On; Take Your Time	4/20/58	39
Br 55072	Think It Over; Fool's Paradise	5/27/58	27 / 58
D 30650	Girl On My Mind; Ting-A-Ling	6/23/58	
C 62006	Early In The Morning; Now We're One	7/5/58	31
Br 55094	It's So Easy; Lonesome Tears	9/12/58	82
C 62017	Real Wild Child; Oh You Beautiful Doll — Ivan	9/26/58	68
C 62051	Heartbeat; Well All Right	11/5/58	
C 62074	It Doesn't Matter Anymore; Raining In My Heart	1/5/59	13 / 88
C 62134	Peggy Sue Got Married; Crying, Waiting, Hoping	7/20/59	
C 62210	True Love Ways; That Makes It Tough	6/29/60	
C 62329	Reminiscing; Wait 'Til The Sun Shines, Nellie	8/20/62	
C 62352	Bo Diddley; True Love Ways	4/1/63	
C 62369	Brown Eyed Handsome Man; Wishing	7/29/63	
C 62390	Rock Around With Ollie Vee; I'm Gonna Love You Too	1/6/64	
C 62407	Maybe Baby; Not Fade Away	4/27/64	
C 62448	What To Do; Slippin' And Slidin'	3/15/65	
C 62554	Rave On; Early In The Morning	7/22/68	
C 62558	Love Is Strange; You're The One	3/17/69	
C 65618	That'll Be The Day; I'm Lookin' For Someone To Love	1/73	
MCA 60000	That'll Be The Day; I'm Looking For Someone To Love	1/73	
MCA 60004	Peggy Sue; Everyday	1/73	
MCA 40905	It Doesn't Matter Anymore; Peggy Sue	5/78	

Extended Play Singles (E.P.s)

(ED = Decca; EB = Brunswick; EC = Coral)

ED 2575 — That'll Be The Day
That'll Be The Day; Blue Days, Black Nights; Ting-A-Ling; You Are My One Desire

EB 71036 — The Chirping Crickets
I'm Looking For Someone To Love; That'll Be The Day; Not Fade Away; Oh Boy!

EB 71038 — The Sound Of The Crickets
Maybe Baby; Rock Me My Baby; Send Me Some Lovin'; Tell Me How

EC 81169 — Listen To Me
Listen To Me Everyday; I'm Gonna Love You Too; Peggy Sue

EC 81182 — The Buddy Holly Story
Early In The Morning; Heartbeat; It Doesn't Matter Anymore; Raining In My Heart

EC 81191 — Peggy Sue Got Married
Peggy Sue Goe Married; Crying, Waiting, Hoping; Learning The Game; That Makes It Tough

EC 81193 — Brown Eyed Handsome Man
Brown Eyed Handsome Man; Bo Diddley; True Love Ways; Wishing

ALBUMS/CD's

BR = Brunswick; C = Coral;
D = Decca; VL = Vocalion; MCA = MCA.

Br 54038 The Chirping Crickets   November 1957
(Re-released in 1962 as *Buddy Holly and the Crickets*, C 57405/757405).
Oh Boy!; Not Fade Away; You've Got Love; Maybe Baby; It's Too Late; Tell Me How; That'll Be The Day; I'm Lookin' For Someone To Love; An Empty Cup; Send Me Some Lovin'; Rock Me My Baby; Last Night.

C 57210 Buddy Holly   March 1958
I'm Gonna Love You Too; Peggy Sue; Look At Me; Listen To Me; Valley Of Tears; Ready Teddy; Everyday; Mailman, Bring Me No More Blues; Words Of Love; You're So Square; Rave On; Little Baby.

D 8707 That'll Be The Day   April 1958
(Re-released in 1967 as *The Great Buddy Holly*, MCAC-737 later renumbered as MCA 20101 with all of the cuts listed below included, except for Ting-A-Ling).
You Are My One Desire; Blue Days, Black Nights; Modern Don Juan; Rock Around With Ollie Vee; Ting-A-Ling; Girl On My Mind; That'll Be The Day; Love Me; I'm Changing All Those Changes; Don't Come Back Knocking; Midnight Shift.

C 57279/75279 The Buddy Holly Story   March 1959
Raining In My Heart; Early In The Morning; Peggy Sue; Maybe Baby; Everyday; Rave On; That'll Be The Day; Heartbeat; Think It Over; Oh Boy!; It's So Easy; It Doesn't Matter Anymore.

C 57326 The Buddy Holly Story, Volume 2   March 1960
Peggy Sue Got Married; Well All Right; What To Do; That Makes It Tough; Now We're One; Take Your Time; Crying, Waiting, Hoping; True Love Ways; Learning The Game; Little Baby; Moondreams; That's What They Say.

C 57426/757426 Reminiscing   February 1963
Reminiscing; Slippin' And Slidin'; Bo Diddley; Wait 'Til The Sun Shines, Nellie; Baby, Won't You Come Out Tonight; Brown Eyed Handsome Man; Because I Love You; It's Not My Fault; I'm Gonna Set My Foot Down; I'm Changing All Those Changes; Rock-A-Bye-Rock.

C 57450/75450 Showcase   May 1964
Shake, Rattle and Roll; Rock Around With Ollie Vee; Honky Tonk; I Guess I Was Just A Fool; Ummm, Oh Yeah (Dearest); You're The One; Blue Suede Shoes; Come Back Baby; Rip It Up; Love's Made A Fool Of You; Gone; Girl On My Mind.

C 57463/757463 Holly In The Hills   January 1965
I Wanna Play House With You; Door To My Heart; Fool's Paradise; I Gambled My Heart; What To Do; Wishing; Down The Line; Soft Place In My Heart; Lonesome Tears; Gotta Get You Near Me Blues; Flower Of My Heart; You And I Are Through.

C CXB-8/7CXSB-8 The Best of Buddy Holly   April 1966
Peggy Sue; Blue Suede Shoes; Learning The Game; Brown Eyed Handsome Man; Everyday; Maybe Baby; Early In The Morning; Ready Teddy; It's Too Late; What To Do; Rave On; True Love Ways; It Doesn't Matter Anymore; Crying, Waiting, Hoping; Moondreams; Rock Around With Ollie Vee; Raining In My Heart; Bo Diddley; That'll Be The Day; I'm Gonna Love You Too; Peggy Sue Got Married; Shake, Rattle And Roll; That Makes It Tough; Wishing.

C 757492 Buddy Holly's Greatest Hits   March 1967
Peggy Sue; True Love Ways; Bo Diddley; What To Do; Learning The Game; It Doesn't Matter Anymore; That'll Be The Day; Oh Boy!; Early In The Morning; Brown Eyed Handsome Man; Everyday; Maybe Baby.

C 757504 Giant   January 1969
Love Is Strange; Good Rockin' Tonight; Blue Monday; Have You Ever Been Lonely; Slippin' And Slidin'; You're The One; Dearest; Smokey Joe's Cafe; Ain't Got No Home; Holly Hop.

VL 73923 Good Rockin'   1971
I Wanna Play House With You; Baby, I Don't Care; Little Baby; Ting-A-Ling; Take Your Time; Down The Line; Now We're One; Words Of Love; That's What They Say; You And I Are Through.

D DXSE7-207 Buddy Holly: A Rock And Roll Collection
   August 1972
(Later renumbered as MCA 2-4009)
Rave On; Tell Me How; Peggy Sue Got Married; Slippin' And Slidin'; Oh Boy!; Not Fade Away; Bo Diddley; What To Do; Heartbeat; Well All Right; Words Of Love; Love's Made A Fool Of You; Reminiscing; Lonesome Tears; Listen To Me; Maybe Baby; Down The Line; That'll Be The Day; Peggy Sue; Brown Eyed Handsome Man; You're So Square; Crying, Waiting, Hoping; Ready Teddy; It Doesn't Matter Anymore.

MCA 1484 Buddy Holly/Crickets 20 Golden Greats   May 1978
That'll Be The Day; Peggy Sue; Words Of Love; Everyday; Not Fade Away; Oh Boy!; Maybe Baby; Listen To Me; Heartbeat; Think It Over; It Doesn't Matter Anymore; It's So Easy; Well All Right; Rave On; Raining In My Heart; True Love Ways; Peggy Sue Got Married; Bo Diddley; Brown Eyed Handsome Man; Wishing.

MCA 6-80000 The Complete Buddy Holly   January 1981
Gotta Get You Near Me Blues; Soft Place In My Heart; Door To My Heart; Flower Of My Heart; Baby It's Love; Memories; Queen Of The Ballroom; I Gambled My Heart; You And I Are Through; Gone; Have You Ever Been Lonely; Down The Line; Brown Eyed Handsome Man; Bo Diddley; Good Rockin' Tonight; Rip It Up; Blue Monday; Honky Tonk; Blue Suede Shoes; Shake Rattle & Roll; Ain't Got No Home;

Holly Hop; Baby Let's Play House; I'm Gonna Set My Foot Down; Baby Won't You Come Out Tonight; Changing All Those Changes; Rock-A-Bye Rock; It's Not My Fault; I Guess I Was Just A Fool; Love Me; Don't Come Back Knockin'; Midnight Shift; Blue Days — Black Nights; Rock Around With Ollie Vee; I'm Changing All Those Changes; That'll Be The Day; Girl On My Mind; Ting-A-Ling; Because I Love You; Rock Around With Ollie Vee; Modern Don Juan; You Are My One Desire; That'll Be The Day; I'm Lookin' For Someone To Love; Last Night; Maybe Baby; Words Of Love; Peggy Sue; Everyday; Mailman, Bring Me No More Blues; Listen To Me; I'm Gonna Love You Too; Not Fade Away; Ready Teddy; Oh Boy!; Tell Me How; Maybe Baby; Send Me Some Lovin'; Little Baby; Take Your Time; Rave On; You've Got Love; Valley Of Tears; Rock Me My Baby; Baby I Don't Care; It's Too Late; An Empty Cup; Look At Me; Think It Over; Fool's Paradise; Early In The Morning; Now We're One; Lonesome Tears; Heartbeat; It's So Easy; Well All Right; Love's Made A Fool Of You; Wishing; Reminiscing; Come Back Baby; That's My Desire; True Love Ways; Moondreams; Raining In My Heart; It Doesn't Matter Anymore; Peggy Sue Got Married; Crying, Waiting, Hoping; Learning The Game; That Makes It Tough; What To Do; That's What They Say; Wait 'Til The Sun Shines, Nellie; Umm, Oh Yeah; Smokey Joe's Cafe; Slippin' And Slidin'; Love Is Strange; Slippin' and Slidin'; Learning The Game; Crying, Waiting, Hoping; What To Do; That Makes It Tough; Peggy Sue Got Married; That's What They Say; Dearest; You're The One; Slippin' And Slidin'; Dearest; Love Is Strange; Peggy Sue Got Married; That Makes It Tough; Learning The Game; You're The One; Real Wild Child; Oh You Beautiful Doll; Jole Blon; When Sin Stops; Stay Close To Me; Don't Cha Know; Interview In Topeka, Kansas; Ed Sullivan Show — That'll Be The Day; Peggy Sue; Interview with Ed Sullivan; Interview with Alan Freed; Interview with Dick Clark.

MCA-27059 For The First Time Anywhere　　　January 1983
I'm Gonna Set My Foot Down; Changing All Those Changes; Rock-A-Bye Rock; Maybe Baby; Bo Diddley; Because I Love You; That's My Desire; It's Not My Fault; Baby Let's Play House.

MCA CD-5540 From The Original Tapes　　　January 1985
Peggy Sue; Maybe Baby; Everyday; Rave On; That'll Be The Day; Heartbeat; Oh Boy!; It Doesn't Matter Anymore; Listen To Me; Think It Over; Well All Right; True Love Ways; Rock Around With Ollie Vee; Not Fade Away; Listen To Me; Think It Over; I'm Looking For Someone To Love; Words Of Love; Reminiscing.

Hanging out on the cycles between tours

Joe, Jerry, Buddy on new Triumph motorcycles, April 1958

Buddy Holly Week & Paul McCartney

Since it was first held to celebrate what would have been the late singer's 40th birthday, "Buddy Holly Week" has established itself as an important and fun-packed event in the annual calendar of pop music events. Important because it serves as a reminder, to both public and music business alike, of the great talent that was Buddy Holly, and also because Holly's following is as big now as it was when he perished in an air crash on February 3, 1959.

Holly's tragically premature death (he was only 22) robbed rock 'n' roll of one of its most innovative talents, but thanks to Paul McCartney, Holly's music lives on.

McCartney acquired the Buddy Holly song catalogue in 1975, but his interest in Buddy's music extended back to the 1950s when — along with millions of other teenagers — Paul rocked along to classic Buddy Holly and the Crickets' songs. The Holly influence continued into the '60s when the Beatles recorded Buddy's *"Crying, Waiting, Hoping"* (which was never released) and included his *"Words Of Love"* on the 1964 Lp *"Beatles For Sale."* (U.K.) and *"Beatles VI"* (U.S.).

Paul McCartney instigated the first "Buddy Holly Week" in September of 1976 to commemorate what would have been the singer's 40th birthday. At a special luncheon, Holly's music mentor Norman Petty was the guest of honor (guests included Elton John, Eric Clapton, Phil Manzanera, Brian May, Andy McKay, Steve Harley). In recognition of his efforts in keeping Holly's name alive, Norman Petty presented McCartney with a pair of Holly's cufflinks.

Subsequently, "Buddy Holly Week" has become a time for celebration in the U.K. and the U.S. with different special activities and contests planned for each year. In 1977, the Crickets were flown in to play a concert at the Gaumont in Kilburn before a star-studded audience which included Ronnie Wood and Mick Jagger (whose first big hit, *"Not Fade Away,"* was a Holly tune). It was a very nostalgic event, as it was the same venue they had played with Holly during their only British tour 18 years prior.

In 1978, the "Week" was climaxed by a midnight showing of the film, *"The Buddy Holly Story,"* attended by many pop music luminaries, who celebrated at a gala party prior to the premiere. The Crickets returned in '79 and were joined before an SRO house by Bob Montgomery (Buddy's first singing partner), Don Everly, Albert Lee, Rick Gretch, Denny Laine and Paul and Linda McCartney. Maria Elena Diaz, Holly's widow, also attended and spoke fondly of McCartney's close involvement with Holly's music. "...He told me that Holly had more influence on his early songwriting than any other singer, and he thought that more should be done to keep his memory alive," she related.

Other "Buddy Holly Weeks" have included a Fan Fair, a Buddy Holly portrait art contest, a Rock 'N' Roll Dance Championship and, of course, a myriad of concerts and films. The MPL Buddy Holly Weeks are strictly non-profit making ventures. Admission to the various events is either free or with a purely nominal charge. All the badges, tee-shirts, souvenirs and stickers are given away free to fans.

The memory of Buddy Holly is kept alive by the timeless quality of his music, and by Paul McCartney's dedication in preserving that memory.

Paraphrased and quoted from "Buddy's Week 1976-80" by Chris White in the fanzine "Club Sandwich" 1980 No. 21, and from "Buddy Holly Week — America '83" a PR folder from MPL.

Letts
gets you through

KS2 GRAMMAR & PUNCTUATION
SATs SUCCESS
TOPIC WORKBOOK

Ages 7–9

KS2 GRAMMAR & PUNCTUATION SATs
TOPIC WORKBOOK

LAURA GRIFFITHS

About this book

Grammar and punctuation

Grammar and punctuation are a key focus of the new primary curriculum. They are crucial English skills that will enable your child to communicate effectively in school and in later life. Developing these skills will help your child to convey clear and accurate information when speaking and writing.

This book separates grammar from punctuation and breaks them down topic by topic, offering clear explanations and practice at each step. It will also aid preparation for the Key Stage 2 **English Grammar, Punctuation and Spelling** test.

Features of the book

- The *Key to grammar* and *Key to punctuation* sections introduce each topic through concise explanations and clear examples.

- *Practice activities* include a variety of tasks to see how well your child has grasped each concept.

- *Test your grammar* and *Test your punctuation* provide focused questions after both sections.

- A *mixed test* at the end of the book helps to cement your child's overall understanding of the grammar and punctuation topics covered.

- *Answers* are in a pull-out booklet at the centre of the book.

Grammar and punctuation tips

- Spend time reading and looking through books (both fiction and non-fiction) asking your child to identify examples of different types of grammar and punctuation. For example, play 'finding an adjective' or 'spotting speech marks', or talk about why a new paragraph has started.

- Encourage your child to write by making diaries, recipe cards, stories and letters together. Encourage them to use the correct punctuation in their own writing.

- Make grammar and punctuation fun. For example, play games like *I spy* but start with: 'I am thinking of a noun beginning with…' or a charades-type game where your child can act out an adverb.

Contents

Grammar

Alphabetical order	4
What is a sentence?	6
Verbs	8
Nouns	10
Nouns – singular and plural	12
Proper and collective nouns	14
Phrases	16
Clauses	18
Pronouns	20
Verbs – which tense?	22
Future tense	24
Irregular verbs	26
Was or were?	28
Did or done?	30
Prepositions	32
Adjectives 1	34
Adjectives 2	36
Adverbs 1	38
Adverbs 2	40
Determiners	42
Conjunctions	44
Time connectives	46
Test your grammar	48

Punctuation

Full stops	50
Exclamation marks	52
Question marks	54
Capital letters	56
Commas in a list	58
Direct speech 1	60
Direct speech 2	62
Paragraphs	64
Test your punctuation	66

Mixed practice questions

Mixed test	68

Answers

Answers (centre pull-out)	1–8

Alphabetical order

Key to grammar

There are 26 letters in the alphabet:

a b c d e f g h i j k l m n o p q r s t u v w x y z

The vowels are **a**, **e**, **i**, **o** and **u**. The remaining letters are **consonants**.

Sometimes words need to be put into **alphabetical order** (for instance, last names in a class register). To do this you need to look at the first letter of each word.

cat   **d**og   **m**ouse

If there are two words with the same first letter, the second letter is used, then the next one, and so on.

cat   **co**w   **do**g   **du**ck

Practice activities

1. Fill in the missing letters in the alphabet.

   a) a ____ c d e ____ g h i j ____ l m n ____ p q ____ s t u v ____ x ____ ____

   b) f g ____ i j k ____

   c) ____ ____ ____ ____ z

Alphabetical order

2. Look at the pictures. Write them in alphabetical order on the line below.

aeroplane

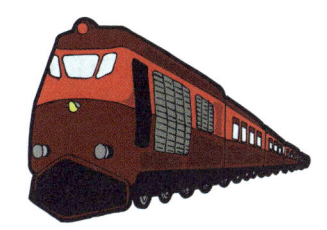

train

bus

car

_____

3. Look at the lists of words. Rewrite them in alphabetical order.

   a) football, tennis, cricket, swimming

   _____

   b) cheese, ham, tuna, jam, egg

   _____

   c) shorts, trousers, skirt, vest, jacket, shoes

   _____

What is a sentence?

Key to grammar

A sentence is a sequence of words that makes sense.

A sentence usually has a **subject** (generally something or someone who is doing something) and a **verb** (a doing or being word).

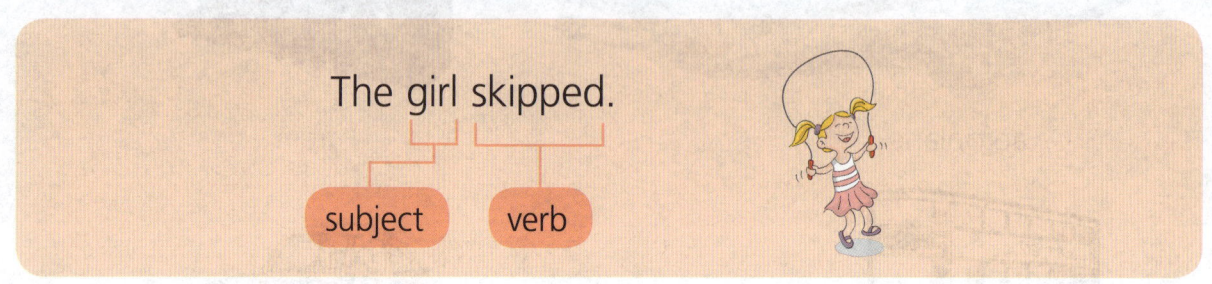

The girl skipped.
subject   verb

Sentences can be made longer by adding more detail or linking sentences using joining words.

There are different types of sentence:

Type	Definition	End punctuation
Statement	A sentence that gives information.	full stop (.)
Question	A sentence that needs an answer.	question mark (?)
Exclamation	A sentence that shows an emotion.	exclamation mark (!)
Command	A sentence that tells someone to do something.	full stop (.) or exclamation mark (!)

Practice activities

1. Put one tick in each row to show whether the sentence is a statement or a question.

Sentence		Statement	Question
a)	What would you like for dinner today?		
b)	I can count to 100.		
c)	Did you enjoy your birthday party?		
d)	The dog barked so loudly, he woke us up.		

What is a sentence?

2. Rewrite these sentences putting the words in the correct order so they make sense.

   a) The car red was.
   _____

   b) Have you started book reading your?
   _____

   c) quiet Be!
   _____

   d) like I eating jam toast with on top.
   _____

3. Look at each sentence below and write whether it is a statement, question or command.

   a) When is your birthday? _____
   b) A square has four straight sides. _____
   c) Go away! _____
   d) The weather forecast is for rain tomorrow. _____
   e) Where are you going on holiday? _____
   f) Come back here! _____
   g) Wait there! _____
   h) I think I like it. _____
   i) Did he play well? _____
   j) My favourite fruit is oranges. _____

Verbs

Key to grammar

A verb is a **doing** or a **being** word. It usually describes an action. It tells us what is happening or what will or has happened.

Examples: eat, walk, learn, swim, laugh

Practice activities

1. Look at the pictures and write the verb each picture is showing.

   a) _____

   b) _____

   c) _____

   d) _____

2. Underline the verb in each sentence.

   a) Mrs Jones cooks tasty meals.

   b) Cinderella dances with Prince Charming at the ball.

   c) The shop sells lots of clothes.

   d) My brother listens to his music on the computer.

Verbs

3. Circle all the verbs.

eat	sleep	stretch	orange

climb	tail

jump	drink

ears	food	pounce

4. Write three verbs to show what each animal below can do.

a)

_____
_____
_____

b)

_____
_____
_____

c)

_____
_____
_____

d)

_____
_____
_____

Nouns

Key to grammar

A **noun** is a word used to refer to a person, animal, place or thing.

Common nouns are general words for people, animals, places and things.

They are not their names but words that tell us what they are.

They do not begin with a capital letter, unless they begin a sentence.

man   girl   dog   horse   station
hotel   planet   chair   pencil   moon

Practice activities

1. Look at the pictures and write the common noun.

   a)

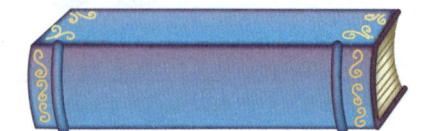

   b)

   c)

   d)

Nouns

2. Circle the common noun in each sentence.

   a) The bird flew away.

   b) We are at the airport.

   c) I brushed my teeth.

   d) The girl jumped high.

3. Circle **all** the common nouns in each sentence.

   a) She wiped the table with the dirty cloth.

   b) Sarah went to the shops and bought some bread and milk.

   c) Alex washed the car and used a bucket, water and two sponges.

   d) The boys played cricket in the park after school.

   e) Their mum asked them to tidy their bedrooms because there were too many toys on the floor.

   f) He licked the ice cream before it melted.

4. Choose a common noun from the box below to fill in the gaps in the sentences.

beach	school	teacher
sweets	monkey	
bag		shells

   a) The cheeky _____ ate all the bananas.

   b) The sandy _____ was covered with _____.

   c) This morning I was late for _____ and forgot my _____.

   d) Our _____ likes eating _____.

5. Write your own sentence that includes **two** common nouns.

   _____

   _____

Nouns – singular and plural

Key to grammar

Nouns can either be **singular** or **plural.** Singular means one. Plural means more than one.

A **regular** plural noun ends in **s** or **es**.

Sometimes a plural noun can be **irregular** and not end in **s** or **es**.

Regular

Singular	Plural
girl	girls
class	classes

Irregular

Singular	Plural
person	people
man	men

An apostrophe is used to show possession of a singular or plural noun. This is when something belongs to someone or something.

Singular	Plural
The dog**'s** basket	The dogs**'** basket

Practice activities

1. Underline all the **plural** nouns in each sentence below.
    a) The cows were in the field.
    b) The excited astronauts were trying on their new spacesuits.
    c) We are going to the library to listen to stories.
    d) The cats and dogs were making lots of noise because they were frightened of the loud fireworks.
    e) We have sandwiches, crisps, apples and sweets in our picnic today.
    f) There were lots of people waiting at the platform for the next two trains this morning.

Nouns – singular and plural

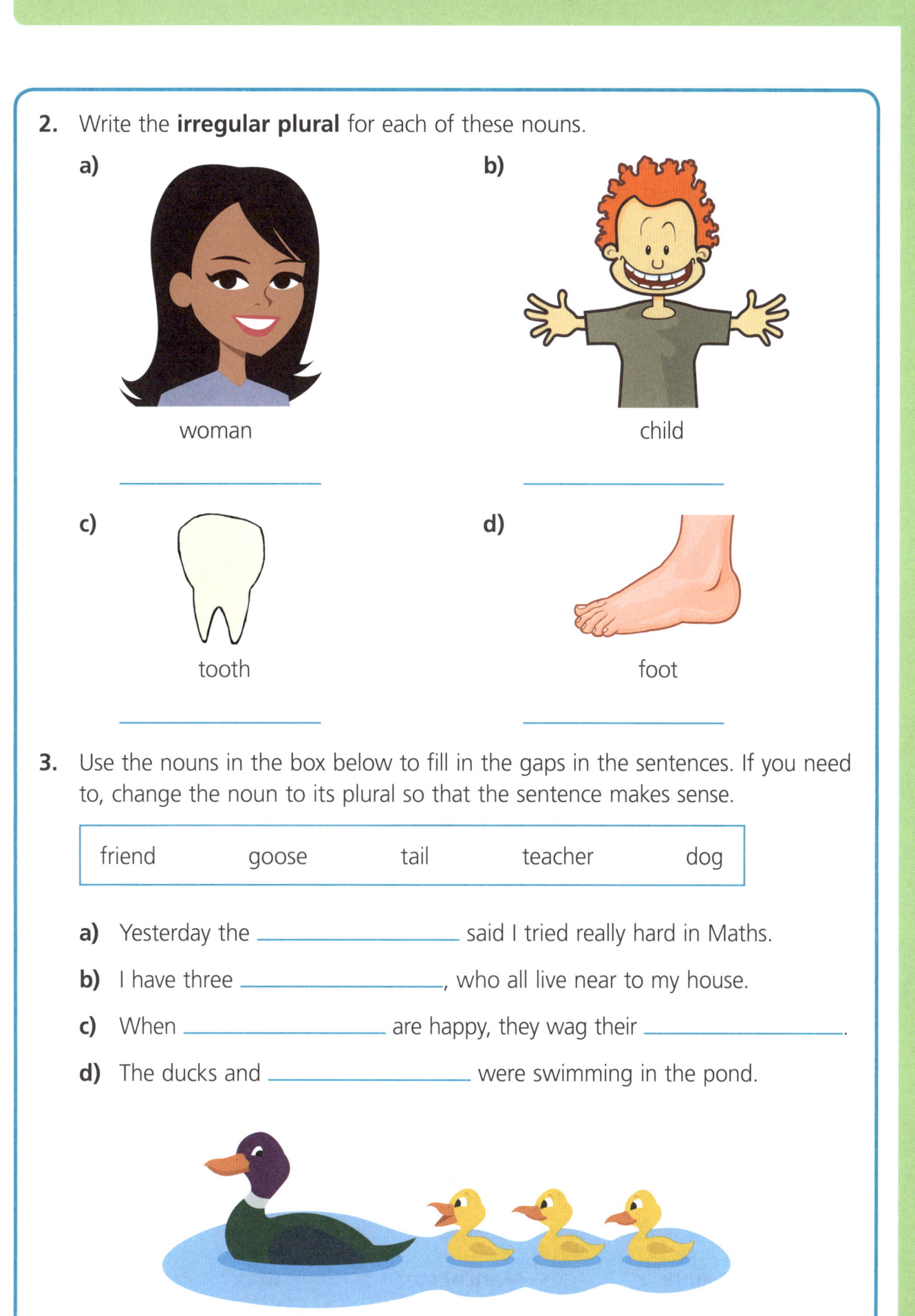

2. Write the **irregular plural** for each of these nouns.

   a) woman _____

   b) child _____

   c) tooth _____

   d) foot _____

3. Use the nouns in the box below to fill in the gaps in the sentences. If you need to, change the noun to its plural so that the sentence makes sense.

   | friend | goose | tail | teacher | dog |

   a) Yesterday the _____ said I tried really hard in Maths.

   b) I have three _____, who all live near to my house.

   c) When _____ are happy, they wag their _____.

   d) The ducks and _____ were swimming in the pond.

Proper and collective nouns

Key to grammar

Proper nouns name a particular person, place, time or event. It is important to remember that they start with a **capital letter**.

Jack	Aisha	America
London	Bond Street	Wednesday
April	Ramadan	Christmas

Collective nouns name a **group** of people, animals or things and do not begin with a capital letter unless they begin a sentence.

a **group** of children   a **litter** of kittens   a **gaggle** of geese

Practice activities

1. Circle the words that are **proper nouns**.

   chocolate   Mrs Smith   April

   presents   Manchester   Max

Proper and collective nouns

2. Choose one of the proper nouns in the box below to add to each sentence.

   | Cardiff | January | Sara |

   a) My birthday is in _____.

   b) _____ likes going to the cinema.

   c) _____ is the capital city of Wales.

3. Draw lines to match each group of animals to the correct **collective noun**.

   a)   herd

   b)   swarm

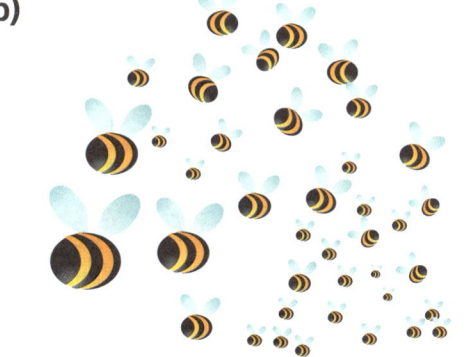

   c)   brood

   d)   flock

Phrases

Key to grammar

A **phrase** is a small group of words that makes up a meaningful unit in a sentence.

A phrase does not usually have a verb and it does not make sense on its own.

The rubbish was put **in the bin**.

The fish were swimming **around the pond**.

Often a single noun could replace a phrase. Phrases are used to add more detail.

The **lucky, little girl** won a prize.

This could simply have said, "The girl won a prize." The words "lucky, little" add more detail.

Practice activities

1. What word type is **not** usually found in phrases? Circle one.

    verb   noun   adjective   adverb

Phrases

2. Underline the phrase in each of these sentences.

   a) My friend's cat likes jumping.

   b) We ate dinner in the kitchen.

   c) I drank a cup of warm tea.

   d) Alex ran along the beach.

   e) Kara's pink bedroom was messy.

   f) He walked down the path.

   g) We can't go shopping in the heavy rain.

3. Choose a phrase below to complete each of the sentences.

of dirty plates	at the park	after lunch
deep and cold	upside down	small and quiet

   a) Bats hang _____.

   b) The waiter was carrying a pile _____.

   c) The mouse, _____, scuttled away.

   d) The sea is _____.

   e) We played football _____.

   f) Bo finished his homework _____.

4. Read the phrase at the start of each sentence and write a suitable ending.

   a) After a long time, _____

   _____

   b) The pretty, white snowflakes _____

   _____

Clauses

Key to grammar

A **main clause** is a sequence of words creating a single idea that makes sense on its own.

It has a verb and a subject.

The girl danced at the show.

subject   verb

A **subordinate clause** is still one idea, but does **not** make sense on its own. A subordinate clause needs a main clause. Together they make a **complex sentence**.

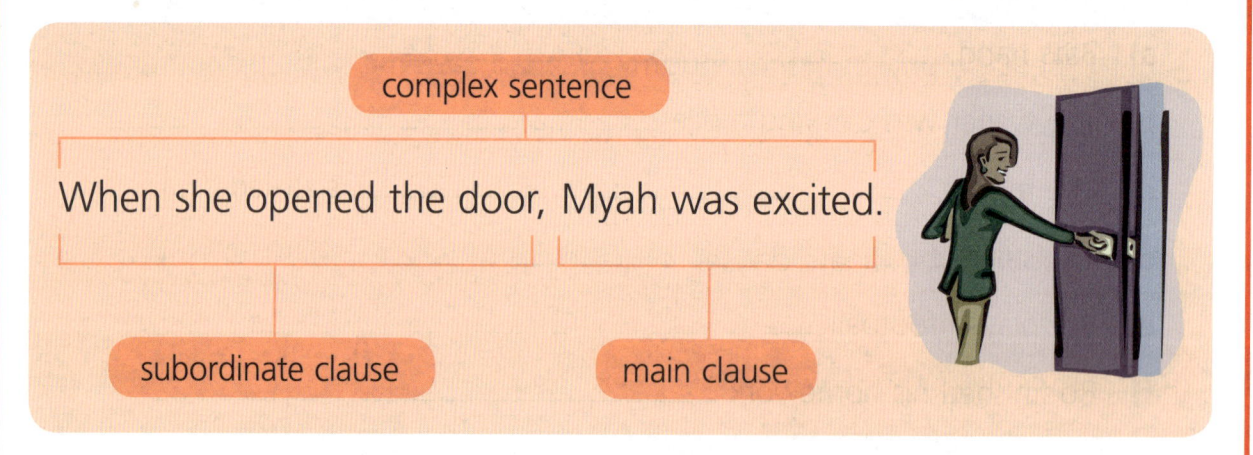

complex sentence

When she opened the door, Myah was excited.

subordinate clause   main clause

Subordinate clauses can start with words such as:

after	although	as
because	before	if
since	that	until
when	which	while	who

Clauses

Practice activities

1. Choose the correct subordinate clause from the boxes below to fill in the gaps in the sentences.

   | even though she had cried | | As her dinner was ready |

   | because he was late |

   a) Eric ran out of the house quickly _____

   b) _____, Tilly opened the kitchen door and sat down at the table.

   c) The dentist gave the girl a sticker _____

2. Underline the **main** clause(s) in each sentence.

   a) When the teacher came into the room, we stopped talking.

   b) We went to the park because the sun was shining.

   c) I spent my pocket money, but my grandad gave me some extra money.

   d) Although they are very noisy, the drums are my favourite instrument.

3. Look at each picture and write a complex sentence for each one using a main clause and a subordinate clause.

   a)

   b)

Pronouns

Key to grammar

A **pronoun** is a word that is used to replace a noun. Pronouns are often used so that the noun is not repeated and to make our writing more interesting.

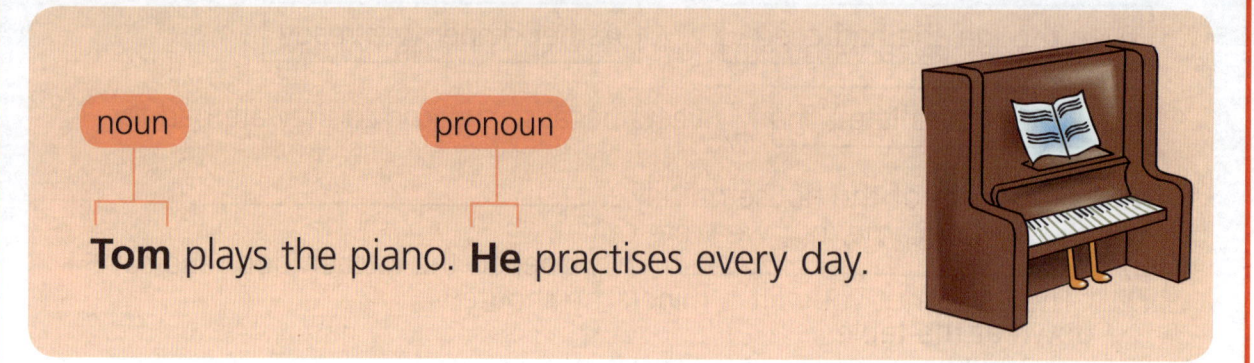

noun — **Tom** plays the piano. pronoun — **He** practises every day.

Some common pronouns are:

I, me, mine
you, yours
he, him, his
she, her, hers

it, its
we, us, ours
they, them, theirs

Practice activities

1. Put a circle around all the pronouns.

he	them	cat	Mrs
Matthew	walking	John	car
she	it	chair	I
house	Sophia	us	snake

20

Pronouns

2. Underline the pronouns in each sentence.

   a) Charlie was tired, so **he** went upstairs to bed.

   b) A spider crawled up the chair. **It** was large and black.

   c) Rebecca played with some toys while **she** was on holiday.

   d) Bethan doesn't eat many sweets because **she** knows **they** are bad for the teeth.

   e) The builder came, but **we** were out.

   f) "The ball is not **yours**. **It** is **mine**!" **he** shouted.

3. Use the pronouns below to complete the story extract.

I	them	they	you

   An old man on the point of death called his sons to give them some advice. He told them to bring in a bundle of sticks, and said to the eldest son:

   "Break it."

   The son really strained but was unable to break the bundle. The other sons tried too, but none of _____ could do it.

   "Untie the bundle," said the father, "and each of _____ take a stick."

   When _____ each had a stick, he said to them:

   "Now, break them," and each stick broke easily.

   Their father then asked: "You see what _____ mean?"

4. Rewrite the sentence replacing the words in bold with a pronoun.

   Dexter read a long book even though **Dexter** found **the long book** difficult.

   _____

   _____

21

Verbs – which tense?

Key to grammar

A **verb** is a doing or being word. Verbs change with different tenses.
- The **past tense** describes something that has already happened.
- The **present tense** is what is happening now.
- The **future tense** refers to what will happen in the future.
- The **present perfect tense** describes something that began in the past but was completed in the present (using the present tense of the verb 'have').

Verb	Present	Past	Future	Present perfect
jump	I jump	I jumped	I will jump	I have jumped

Practice activities

1. Underline the verb(s) in each sentence.
   a) Toby shouted at his brother.
   b) The monkey grabbed a large bunch of bananas.
   c) The children will eat their dinner in the hall.
   d) We are riding our bikes to the park.
   e) Emma and Tina danced at the disco last night.
   f) I drink water because it keeps me healthy.
   g) Charlotte cried when she fell off her scooter.

Verbs – which tense?

2. Fill in the gaps in the table to show how each verb changes tense.

Verb	Present	Past	Future
laugh	she laughs	she laughed	she will laugh
walk		you walked	you will walk
play	he plays		
talk		we talked	
skip	they skip		they will skip

3. Write these sentences again, changing the verbs so that they are in the **past tense.**

a) I work hard at school.

_____

b) I tidy my bedroom.

_____

c) We jump in muddy puddles.

_____

d) I play with my toys.

_____

4. Circle the correct form of the verb in the following sentences, which use the **present perfect tense**.

a) He **has / have** celebrated his birthday.

b) We have **open / opened** our presents.

c) I **has / have** blown out the candles.

Future tense

Key to grammar

The **future tense** tells us about things that will happen in the future.

When verbs are written in the future tense, we often add **will** or **shall** before the verb.

I **will** sing in the concert.

I **shall** run in the race.

Practice activities

1. Underline the verbs paired with **will** or **shall** in each sentence.

   a) The sports day will start at four o'clock.

   b) The girls will play football tomorrow.

   c) Next week, I shall walk to school.

   d) Tomorrow, I will run to school.

2. Fill in the gaps in the table using **will**.

Present tense	Future tense
I eat.	I will eat.
We cook.	
They sit.	

Future tense

3. Some friends are going on holiday next week. Look at the pictures of everything they will do and write a sentence for each in the future tense.

a)

b)

_____

_____

c)

d)

_____

_____

4. Circle the correct form of the verb for each sentence.

a) On holiday, I will **play / played** on the beach.

b) I will **ate / eat** my dinner in the kitchen.

c) The boys in my class will **learnt / learn** to play cricket.

d) My sister will **take / took** her exams next month.

e) The clown will **juggle / juggles** ten balls.

f) The whales will **dove / dive** soon.

Irregular verbs

Key to grammar

Most verbs are **regular** and can be changed easily from the present to the past tense by doing little more than adding **ed**.

Present tense	Past tense
I walk	I walk**ed**
I laugh	I laugh**ed**
I open	I open**ed**

Other verbs are **irregular** and don't follow this rule.

Present tense	Past tense
I am	I was
I speak	I spoke
I eat	I ate

Practice activities

1. Draw a line to match the correct present and past tense verb.

    a) break   heard

    b) know   did

    c) go   swam

    d) ride   took

    e) do   rode

    f) take   went

    g) swim   knew

    h) hear   broke

Irregular verbs

2. Circle the correct form of the verb, making sure that each sentence is in the **past** tense.

    a) The aeroplane **flies / flew** very high.

    b) The monkey **have / had** five bananas.

    c) Jack **sold / sell** the cow for some magic beans.

    d) The beanstalk **grow / grew** very high.

    e) The magician, outside the circus, **stood / stands** very still.

    f) The boy **sat / sit** on the chair.

3. Write the verbs in the correct tense to complete this table.

Present tense	Past tense
think	thought
	grew
find	
make	
	said
	blew

4. Choose one of the verbs from the table above and use it to write a sentence in the past tense.

    _____

    _____

5. Circle the words below to which **ed** can be added.

    play   drive   cook   teach

Was or were?

Key to grammar

Most mistakes in grammar are because the verb and the noun are not matched correctly.

For instance, sometimes **was** and **were** get muddled.

As a rule, if the subject is **singular** use **was,** except when the subject is **you**.

If the subject is **plural**, or the word **you** is used, put **were**.

Singular	Plural	You (singular or plural)
He **was** happy.	They **were** happy.	You [the boy] **were** happy.
The boy **was** happy.	The boys **were** happy.	You [the boys] **were** happy.

Practice activities

1. Complete these sentences using **was** or **were**.

   a) Rebecca and Varsha _____ baking a cake.

   b) The school gate _____ locked.

   c) The wicked witch _____ nasty to the frog.

   d) You _____ very cross!

   e) The cars _____ stuck in a traffic jam.

   f) It _____ her ballet exam last week.

Was or were?

2. Write **was** or **were** in the gaps so the story is written correctly.

Once upon a time, there _____ a lion lying by a tree. A little mouse _____ running up and down the lion's back, and he _____ beginning to make the lion angry. The lion turned its large head and opened its mouth widely. With its piercing eyes glaring, the lion _____ about to swallow the little mouse in one big gulp.

Just then, the little mouse squeaked, "Please don't eat me! One day you might need me to help you."

The lion laughed but let the little mouse go free. He _____ sure he would never need help from such a small, pathetic creature. Then, one day, three men _____ walking through the forest holding nets. The men _____ trying to catch the lion and swiftly threw a net over the lion's strong body. The lion roared and struggled, but there _____ nothing he could do. He could not escape.

Just then, the little mouse returned to help the lion. He began, very slowly, to gnaw and chew through the net with his sharp teeth. Eventually, the mouse made a hole that _____ wide enough for the lion to escape.

3. Put a circle around the correct word to start each question.

  a) **Was / Were** the girls playing tennis last night?

  b) **Was / Were** it cold on the way to school this morning?

  c) **Was / Were** there any sweets left in the bag?

  d) **Was / Were** the television left on?

Did or done?

Key to grammar

Sometimes **did** and **done** get muddled. The words **has**, **have** or **had** should normally appear before **done**. The examples in the table below should help you.

Past tense	Present perfect tense	Past perfect tense
I **did** it.	I **have done** it.	I **had done** it.
You **did** it.	You **have done** it.	You **had done** it.
He/she/it **did** it.	He/she/it **has done** it.	He/she/it **had done** it.
We **did** it.	We **have done** it.	We **had done** it.
They **did** it.	They **have done** it.	They **had done** it.

Practice activities

1. In each sentence circle the correct form of the verb.

    a) They **done** / **did** it together.

    b) Ella had **did** / **done** very well in her badminton match.

    c) I **did** / **done** all my homework.

    d) They **done** / **did** the cooking together.

Did or done?

2. Write **did** or **done** in the following sentences

   a) What _____ you buy from the shops?

   b) They've _____ very well.

   c) We've _____ the painting carefully.

   d) _____ you catch the bus or the train?

   e) We've _____ all our activities.

   f) I _____ my best!

3. Draw a line to match the correct ending to the start of each sentence.

   a) I have done   very well in their swimming lesson.

   b) We did   a handstand together.

   c) They did   nothing wrong!

4. Write two sentences of your own using **did** and **done** correctly.

   a) _____

   b) _____

31

Prepositions

Key to grammar

Prepositions are words that describe the relationship between one thing and another. They link nouns or pronouns to other words in a sentence.

> The dog is **in** his basket.
> The dog is **next to** the cat.
> The dog is **under** his blanket.

Prepositions show the relationship between things in terms of **place** or **time**.

> My dad laughed **during** the show.
> (*time*)

> My dad walked **over** the bridge.
> (*place*)

Practice activities

1. Underline the preposition in each sentence.
    a) The dirty, old dog ran into the house.
    b) Jessica sat next to her friend.
    c) Sam jumped in muddy puddles.
    d) The football team ran around the pitch.
    e) The ant is under the rock.

2. Put a circle around the prepositions below.

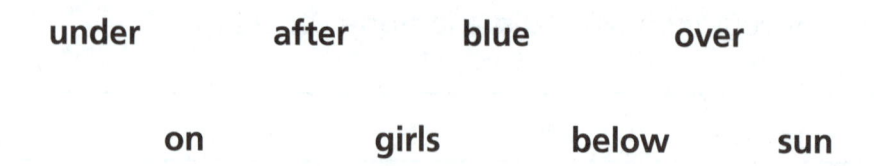

    under   after   blue   over

        on   girls   below   sun

Prepositions

3. Look at each picture and write a sentence using a preposition to describe it.

a)

_____
_____
_____

b)

_____
_____
_____

c)

_____
_____
_____

d)

_____
_____
_____

4. Circle one preposition to make each sentence correct.

a) I need to post the letter **into** / **onto** the postbox.

b) Suzie lives **around** / **next to** the park.

c) In English, Amy sits **behind** / **inside** me.

d) The boy hit the cricket ball **out of** / **over** the fence.

Adjectives 1

Key to grammar

Adjectives tell us more about a noun. Adjectives are **describing** words.

> the **green** grass   a **tall** man
>
> a **quiet** mouse   the **noisy** children

Comparative adjectives are used to compare two nouns.
- The dog is **bigger** than the cat.
- The green bus is **quicker** than the red one.

Superlative adjectives compare **more** than two nouns.
- Baby Bear's porridge was hot. Mummy Bear's porridge was hotter, but Daddy Bear's porridge was the **hottest.**
- My football team is the **greatest**.
- My car is fast. My dad's car is faster, but my brother's car is the **fastest**.

Practice activities

1. Look at the picture and write **three** adjectives to describe each one:

a)

b)

c)

d)

e)

Adjectives 1

2. Make the adjectives in brackets into **comparative** adjectives.

    a) My teacher is (kind) _____ than the others.

    b) The playground is (large) _____ than my garden.

    c) Our new baby is (noisy) _____ than me.

    d) Monday was (hot) _____ than Tuesday.

    e) The DVD I watched was (funny) _____ than the TV programme.

3. Write the correct adjective in the table below.

Adjective	Comparative	Superlative
hot	hotter	hottest
	prettier	
		tallest

4. **Underline** the **comparative** adjective and put a **circle** around the **superlative** adjective in each sentence.

    a) In my class, Sophie is taller than James, but Lucy is the tallest.

    b) The big swimming pool is colder than the small one, but the outside pool is the coldest.

    c) My music is louder than my sister's, although my brother's music is the loudest.

    d) After the games, the cricketer was dirty, the footballer was dirtier, but the rugby player was the dirtiest of all.

    e) The red car was faster than the blue car, but the silver car was the fastest and won the race.

    f) The tallest sunflower was 50cm longer than mine.

5. Look at the adjectives below. Write another adjective next to each one that has the same meaning.

big		nice	
hot		little	

Adjectives 2

Key to grammar

Whether writing or speaking, **adjectives** can make our sentences more interesting because they add detail and description. For example:

I am going to make sandcastles on the beach.

I am going to make **tall**, **golden** sandcastles on the **hot**, **sandy** beach.

Practice activities

1. Look at the words below. Circle the adjectives.

   green light   old clothes   dirty bus

   delicious cakes   clever boy   soggy paper

2. Underline the adjectives in the paragraph below.

   Yesterday, we went to the fair. It was amazing! There were bright, flashing lights and there was very loud music. I liked the big rides the best. The scariest ride was the ghost train, so I went on that with my dad. At the end of the day, we shared some warm, sticky doughnuts and bought some pink, fluffy candyfloss to take home.

Answers

Pages 4–5

1. **a)** b f k o r w y z
   b) h l
   c) v w x y
2. aeroplane, bus, car, train
3. **a)** cricket, football, swimming, tennis
   b) cheese, egg, ham, jam, tuna
   c) jacket, shoes, shorts, skirt, trousers, vest

Pages 6–7

1. **a)** question **b)** statement **c)** question
   d) statement
2. **a)** The car was red.
   b) Have you started reading your book?
   c) Be quiet!
   d) I like eating toast with jam on top.
3. **a)** question **b)** statement **c)** command
   d) statement **e)** question **f)** command
   g) command **h)** statement **i)** question
   j) statement

Pages 8–9

1. **a)** swim **b)** drive **c)** read/sit **d)** paint
2. **a)** Mrs Jones <u>cooks</u> tasty meals.
   b) Cinderella <u>dances</u> with Prince Charming at the ball.
   c) The shop <u>sells</u> lots of clothes.
   d) My brother <u>listens</u> to music on the computer.
3. eat, sleep, stretch, climb, jump, drink, pounce
4. **a)–d) Accept any appropriate verbs,
      e.g.: a)** run, eat, walk **b)** swim, move, glide **c)** hop, eat, jump **d)** gallop, jump, neigh

Pages 10–11

1. **a)** book **b)** train **c)** house **d)** tiger
2. **a)** bird **b)** airport **c)** teeth **d)** girl
3. **a)** table, cloth
   b) shops, bread, milk
   c) car, bucket, water, sponges
   d) boys, cricket, park, school
   e) mum, bedrooms, toys, floor
   f) ice cream
4. **a)** monkey **b)** beach, shells
   c) school, bag **d)** teacher, sweets
5. **Accept any grammatically correct sentence that includes two common nouns, e.g.:** The **parrot** copied what the **man** said.

Pages 12–13

1. **a)** The <u>cows</u> were in the field.
   b) The excited <u>astronauts</u> were trying on their new <u>spacesuits</u>.
   c) We are going to the library to listen to <u>stories</u>.
   d) The <u>cats</u> and <u>dogs</u> were making lots of noise because they were frightened of the loud <u>fireworks</u>.
   e) We have <u>sandwiches</u>, <u>crisps</u>, <u>apples</u> and <u>sweets</u> in our picnic today.
   f) There were lots of <u>people</u> waiting at the platform for the next two <u>trains</u> this morning.
2. **a)** women **b)** children **c)** teeth **d)** feet
3. **a)** teacher **b)** friends/teachers
   c) dogs, tails **d)** geese

Pages 14–15

1. Mrs Smith, April, Manchester, Max
2. **a)** January **b)** Sara **c)** Cardiff
3. **a)** flock **b)** swarm **c)** herd **d)** brood

Pages 16–17

1. verb
2. **a)** My friend's cat likes jumping.
   b) We ate dinner <u>in the kitchen</u>.
   c) I drank <u>a cup of warm tea</u>.
   d) Alex ran <u>along the beach</u>.
   e) Kara's <u>pink bedroom</u> was messy.
   f) He walked <u>down the path</u>.
   g) We can't go shopping <u>in the heavy rain</u>.
3. **a)** upside down
   b) of dirty plates
   c) small and quiet
   d) deep and cold
   e) at the park
   f) after lunch
4. **a)–b) Accept any suitable and grammatically correct ending to the sentences.**

Pages 18–19

1. **a)** because he was late
   b) As her dinner was ready
   c) even though she had cried
2. **a)** When the teacher came into the room, <u>we stopped talking</u>.
   b) <u>We went to the park</u> because the sun was shining.

1

Answers

c) I spent my pocket money, but my grandad gave me some extra money.
d) Although they are very noisy, the drums are my favourite instrument.

3. **a) Any suitable and grammatically correct complex sentence, e.g.:** The Oak tree, which is the largest in Sherwood Forest, is where Robin Hood once lived.
   b) Any suitable and grammatically correct complex sentence, e.g.: The birthday cake, which had five candles on, was for my sister's party.

Pages 20–21

1. he, them, she, it, I, us
2. a) Charlie was tired, so he went upstairs to bed.
   b) A spider crawled up the chair. It was large and black.
   c) Rebecca played with some toys while she was on holiday.
   d) Bethan doesn't eat many sweets because she knows they are bad for the teeth.
   e) The builder came, but we were out.
   f) "The ball is not yours. It is mine!" he shouted.
3. An old man on the point of death called his sons to give them some advice. He told them to bring in a bundle of sticks, and said to the eldest son:
   "Break it."
   The son really strained but was unable to break the bundle. The other sons tried too, but none of **them** could do it.
   "Untie the bundle," said the father, "and each of **you** take a stick."
   When **they** each had a stick, he said to them:
   "Now, break them," and each stick broke easily. Their father then asked: "You see what **I** mean?"
4. Dexter read a long book even though **he** found it difficult.

Pages 22–23

1. a) Toby shouted at his brother.
   b) The monkey grabbed a large bunch of bananas.
   c) The children will eat their dinner in the hall.
   d) We are riding our bikes to the park.
   e) Emma and Tina danced at the disco last night.
   f) I drink water because it keeps me healthy.
   g) Charlotte cried when she fell off her scooter.

2.
Verb	Present	Past	Future
laugh	she laughs	she laughed	she will laugh
walk	**you walk**	you walked	you will walk
play	he plays	**he played**	**he will play**
talk	**we talk**	we talked	**we will talk**
skip	they skip	**they skipped**	they will skip

3. a) I worked hard at school.
   b) I tidied my bedroom.
   c) We jumped in muddy puddles.
   d) I played with my toys.
4. a) has b) opened c) have

Pages 24–25

1. a) The sports day will start at four o'clock.
   b) The girls will play football tomorrow.
   c) Next week, I shall walk to school.
   d) Tomorrow, I will run to school.

2.
Present tense	Future tense
I eat.	I will eat.
We cook.	**We will cook.**
They sit.	**They will sit.**

3. a) They will swim.
   b) They will surf.
   c) They will dance.
   d) They will sleep.
4. a) play b) eat c) learn d) take e) juggle
   f) dive

Pages 26–27

1. a) break – broke b) know – knew
   c) go – went d) ride – rode
   e) do – did f) take – took
   g) swim – swam h) hear – heard

2

Answers

2. **a)** flew **b)** had **c)** sold
   d) grew **e)** stood **f)** sat

3.
Present tense	Past tense
think	thought
grow	grew
find	**found**
make	**made**
say	said
blow	blew

4. Accept any correct sentence.
5. play; cook

Pages 28–29

1. **a)** were **b)** was **c)** was
   d) were **e)** were **f)** was
2. Once upon a time, there was a lion lying by a tree. A little mouse was running up and down the lion's back, and he was beginning to make the lion angry. The lion turned its large head and opened its mouth widely. With its piercing eyes glaring, the lion was about to swallow the little mouse in one big gulp.
   Just then the little mouse squeaked, "Please don't eat me! One day you might need me to help you."
   The lion laughed but let the little mouse go free. He was sure he would never need help from such a small, pathetic creature. Then, one day, three men were walking through the forest holding nets. The men were trying to catch the lion and swiftly threw a net over the lion's strong body. The lion roared and struggled, but there was nothing he could do. He could not escape.
   Just then the little mouse returned to help the lion. He began, very slowly, to gnaw and chew through the net with his sharp teeth. Eventually, the mouse made a hole that was wide enough for the lion to escape.
3. **a)** Were **b)** Was **c)** Were **d)** Was

Pages 30–31

1. **a)** did **b)** done **c)** did **d)** did
2. **a)** did **b)** done **c)** done
   d) Did **e)** done **f)** did

3. **a)** I have done nothing wrong!
   b) We did a handstand together.
   c) They did very well in their swimming lesson.
4. **a)–b)** Accept any correct sentences using **did** and **done**.

Pages 32–33

1. **a)** The dirty, old dog ran into the house.
   b) Jessica sat next to her friend.
   c) Sam jumped in muddy puddles.
   d) The football team ran around the pitch.
   e) The ant is under the rock.
2. under, after, over, on, below
3. **a)** The book is on the table.
   b) The fox is in / under a box.
   c) The cat is under / beneath the table.
   d) The sun is behind the cloud.
   (**a/an** instead of **the** also correct)
4. **a)** into **b)** next to **c)** behind **d)** over

Pages 34–35

1. **a)–e)** Accept any suitable adjectives, e.g.: **a)** cute, furry, small **b)** big, grey, heavy **c)** long, yellow, bright **d)** sandy, hot, warm **e)** fiery, hot, yellow
2. **a)** kinder **b)** larger **c)** noisier
   d) hotter **e)** funnier

3.
Adjective	Comparative	Superlative
hot	hotter	hottest
pretty	prettier	**prettiest**
tall	**taller**	tallest

4. **a)** taller, ⟨tallest⟩ **b)** colder, ⟨coldest⟩
   c) louder, ⟨loudest⟩ **d)** dirtier, ⟨dirtiest⟩
   e) faster, ⟨fastest⟩ **f)** longer, ⟨tallest⟩
5. **a)–d)** Any adjectives that are synonyms, e.g.

big	large
hot	**warm**

nice	**kind**
little	**small**

Pages 36–37

1. green, old, dirty, delicious, clever, soggy
2. Yesterday, we went to the fair. It was amazing! There were bright, flashing lights and there was very loud music. I liked the big rides the best. The scariest ride was the ghost train, so I went on that with my dad. At the end of the day, we shared some

3

Answers

warm, sticky doughnuts and bought some pink, fluffy candyfloss to take home.
3. **Accept any suitable adjectives.**
4. **a)–b) Accept any suitable adjectives relating to the nouns.**
5. **Accept any appropriate adjectives. For example:** Today was brilliant as it was our school's sports day! The **green** field was covered in **bouncy** balls, bats, **tangled** skipping ropes, **soft** bean bags and many more **fun** games. Our class was split into four teams. I was in the **red** team! Lots of **excited** mums and dads were sitting on **small** chairs, waiting for us to start our activities and races. When the **loud** whistle blew, we were off. Ready, steady, go!

Pages 38–39
1. a) slowly b) fiercely c) loudly
   d) patiently e) carefully, gently f) angrily
2. **Any suitable adverbs, e.g.**

talk	run	drink	dance
quietly	quickly	noisily	beautifully
loudly	smoothly	thirstily	awkwardly

3. At my birthday party, there was a clever magician who waved his wand gently over a special box. He shouted the magic words loudly three times, then asked for a helper from the audience. Excitedly, I put up my hand, and before I could change my mind, the magician had chosen me. I went bravely to the front of the stage and helped him mysteriously produce a floppy-eared, soft, white rabbit. Everyone loved the trick and clapped enthusiastically at the end.
4. a) Before b) sometimes c) outside
   d) Yesterday
5. a) Soon b) loudly c) busily d) Perhaps

Pages 40–41
1. a) On Friday, I walked for half an hour.
   b) I met my friends outside school.
   c) I usually go and visit my grandma on a Wednesday.
   d) Dan ate some chocolate after his tea.
   e) Kosha practised playing the violin every day.
2. a) how often b) where c) when
   d) where and when e) where
3. a) Quickly, the horse galloped down the track.
   b) Swiftly, the bird darted through the sky.
   c) Gently, the little girl stroked the purring cat.
   d) Gracefully, the gymnast flew through the air.
4. **Accept any sentence that makes sense and starts with a fronted adverbial,**
   e.g.: Eagerly, the geese pecked at the bread.

Pages 42–43
1. a) The girl put on a jumper
   b) I need a paint brush.
   c) I had an egg for breakfast.
2. Words starting with a consonant sound under **a**; words starting with a vowel sound under **an**.
3. a) a trumpet b) an elephant
   c) an umbrella d) a game
   e) a holiday f) an insect
4. a) I need to wear **a/the** sunhat when **the** sun is shining.
   b) I saw **an/the** ant crawling along **the** leaves.
   c) When I go to **the** shops, I need to buy **a** loaf of bread.
   d) **The/A** teacher read **a/the** story in assembly this morning.
   e) Alicia had **a** tummy ache after eating too many cakes.
5. a) Paige likes reading **the/a** book about dinosaurs.
   b) I will be back in **an** hour.
   c) **The** animals were waiting to see the vet.

Pages 44–45
1. a) I like oranges, but my sister prefers apples.
   b) I am feeling cold and I have a headache.
   c) My dad said I could have a new bike if I keep my bedroom tidy.
   d) We have a different teacher today because Mrs Power is ill.
2. a) unless b) because c) so d) but e) and
3. **Accept any sentences using the given conjunctions that make sense, e.g.:**
   a) I am hungry because I didn't eat any dinner.

4

Answers

b) I have lots of homework tonight so I can't see my friends.
c) Would you like chicken or fish for tea?
d) We can play outside unless it rains heavily.
e) The children like to go swimming when the weather is hot.

Pages 46–47
1. a) I need to be at school <u>before</u> nine o'clock.
   b) When I make a cake, I read the recipe. <u>Next</u>, I find the ingredients I need.
   c) "You can go and play outside <u>as soon as</u> it has stopped raining," my mum said.
   d) Mr Bull helped our class learn some new songs, <u>then</u> he helped another class.
   e) We have been waiting for the bus to arrive <u>since</u> nine o'clock.
   f) My birthday is in June, <u>then</u> it will be Amy's in July.
   g) <u>When</u> the plane <u>finally</u> arrived in Spain, I was feeling very excited.
2. a) First b) Next c) then d) as soon as e) When f) Meanwhile g) Finally
3. **Accept any sentences that make sense and use the time connectives, e.g.:**
   a) Next I will brush my teeth.
   b) I will tidy my bedroom then play a game.
   c) As soon as it is 8pm, I will go to bed.

Pages 48–49
1. Oh, no! – exclamation
   Where are you going? – question
   The sea was very cold. – statement
   (1 mark for all three correct)
2. put *(1 mark)*
3.

Present tense	Past tense
play	**played**
swim	swam
laugh	laughed
build	**built**
run	**ran**
cry	cried
fall	**fell**

(2 marks for all correct; 1 mark for 3–6 correct)

4. The <u>smartest</u> dog won first prize in the dog show last night. *(1 mark)*
5. Cautiously and carefully, Sam lifted the cakes out of the oven. *(1 mark)*
6. bike, cousin, scooter *(1 mark for all 3 correct)*
7. she *(1 mark)*
8. because *(1 mark)*
9. Everyone is going to the cinema tonight. *(1 mark)*
10. When they were young, <u>the children loved going camping</u>. *(1 mark)*
11. I have done all my homework. *(1 mark)*

Pages 50–51
1. a) I am going to go to After School Club today.
   b) The farmer has lots of animals in his field.
   c) We are going to the seaside tomorrow. I am looking forward to it.
   d) "Help! Help!' they shouted. The children were stuck inside the shed. They couldn't get out.
2. **Accept any suitable sentences about each picture that correctly use a full stop, e.g.:**
   a) My favourite toy is my teddy bear called Big Ted.
   b) I love playing on the swings with my brother.
3. Dear Daddy Bear, Mummy Bear and Baby Bear,
   I am so sorry that I broke into your house. I was very hungry and could see your lovely bowls of porridge cooling on the table. Baby Bear, your porridge was delicious. It tasted just right.
   After eating all the porridge, I decided to have a rest. I didn't mean to break the chair in your living room. I didn't know what to do, so I went upstairs and hid. I loved Baby Bear's bed. It was so comfy! I must have fallen asleep before you came back. You seemed very cross with me so I ran out of your cottage and hid further down the path. I didn't want to get into trouble.
   I hope one day you will forgive me and we can be friends.
   Lots of love, Goldilocks xxx

Answers

4. Dear Goldilocks,
   Thank you for your letter. We accept your apology and hope we can now be friends. Would you like to come round to our cottage again sometime? Maybe we could cook you some tea. Baby Bear would love to play with you in the garden. Please let us know if you would like that too.
   Lots of love, The Three Bears xxx

Pages 52–53

1. Once upon a time, there was a little old lady and a little old man. One day, they decided to bake a gingerbread man, so they made him carefully and then put him in the oven to cook.
   When the Gingerbread Man was ready, the little old lady opened the oven door, but, … oh, no! The Gingerbread Man ran away! Before the little old man and the little old lady had blinked, the Gingerbread Man had run out of the house and was halfway up the road.
   "Run, run as fast as you can! You can't catch me. I'm the Gingerbread Man!"
   "Help!" cried the little old lady to a nearby farmer.
   "Quick, run!" shouted the farmer, "We can catch him!"
   But the Gingerbread Man continued to run, still singing. "Run, run as fast as you can! You can't catch me. I'm the Gingerbread Man!"

2. **Accept any suitable sentences that use an exclamation mark and are grammatically correct, e.g.:**
   a) Ouch! I have hurt my finger!
   b) Stop it! Please don't argue anymore!
   c) Don't touch! The iron is hot!
   d) Quick, run! We can win the race!
   e) Help! Help! I'm stuck in the lift!

3. Go away! – an order
   Ouch! – pain
   Wow! – surprise

Pages 54–55

1. a) Please can someone help me?
   b) Would you like to go to the playground today?
   c) Where is the train station?

2. a) I am going outside to play in the snow.
   b) Are you ready for the race tomorrow?
   c) Which colour do you prefer?
   d) Where are my shoes? I can't find them anywhere.
   e) The children were excited about the school disco.

3. **Accept any suitable questions that are grammatically correct and use the relevant question word, e.g.:**
   a) Where is the bus going?
   b) When would you use a tour bus?
   c) How many levels does the bus have?
   d) What time of day is shown in the picture?
   e) Which is the tallest building?
   f) Have you ever been to London?

Pages 56–57

1. a) december, paul, france, david
   b) i) **D**ecember ii) **P**aul iii) **F**rance iv) **D**avid

2. **T**oday will be a warm, dry day. **I**t will start cloudy in most areas of **E**ngland and **W**ales, but by lunchtime the sun will be shining! **D**evon and **C**ornwall will see the highest temperatures, whereas **L**incolnshire and **Y**orkshire will be the coolest.
   Tonight will remain warm and slightly humid, and tomorrow and **T**hursday we may see some heavy thunderstorms.

3. a) **O**n a **M**onday evening, **L**eah and **K**ate go to choir practice.
   b) **M**y birthday is in **M**arch, but my sister's birthday is in **A**ugust.
   c) **M**r **T**homson's pupils were being very noisy because they were practising a play.
   d) **P**ebbles was a shy cat who didn't like **M**rs **S**tone, the vet.
   e) **O**ur favourite sport is football. **W**e play it every **S**aturday at the park.

Pages 58–59

1. a) I am wearing trousers, a T-shirt, socks and shoes.
   b) My favourite colours are red, blue, green, yellow and silver.
   c) My mum can play the piano, the flute and the clarinet.
   d) I like playing on the swings, slide and roundabout.

Answers

e) My favourite subjects at school are English, music, science and PE.

f) My cousins are called Chloe, Jules, Safa and Joe.

g) On holiday I went to the beach, the swimming pool, the disco and the museum.

2. a) The fish is yellow, blue, green and gold.

    b) My sandwich has ham, cheese, butter and pickle in it.

3. a) I would like some bread, milk, jam, eggs and sugar.

    b) I need apples, oranges, bananas, strawberries and pears.

    c) I must remember to buy some peas, carrots, broccoli, celery and tomatoes.

Pages 60–61

1. a) "Sweep the floors and iron our clothes, Cinderella!" shouted the Ugly Sisters.

    b) "Hurry up with the washing, Cinderella!"

    c) Cinderella whispered to herself, "I would love to wear a pretty dress."

2. a) "How long is it until dinner is ready?" Sam asked.

    b) "What time do you usually go to bed?"

    c) "Please can I go to the park, Mum?" Rachel asked.

    d) "Oh no!" sighed Dad.

    e) "Where would you like to go on holiday?" Mum and Dad asked.

    f) The man next door shouted, "Keep the noise down, please!"

    g) The teacher shouted, "Sit down everyone!"

    h) "Have you eaten all your dinner today?" Mum asked.

3. a) "What time does your party start?" Olivia asked.

    b) "Can I have a drink of water, please?" Radi asked his teacher.

    c) "Go and put your shoes on!" Mum shouted.

Pages 62–63

1. a) "I love going to school," Ben said.

    b) "The train is delayed, so I'm going to be home late," Dad grumbled.

    c) "Can you tell me where the nearest shop is, please?"

    d) "Ouch!" Mrs Baker shouted. "I've hurt my toe!"

2. a) "What time are you leaving?" I asked my friends.

    b) "We will be going at about two o'clock," they replied.

    c) "Can I come too?" I asked.

    d) "Of course you can."

3. a) "Hurry up! You'll be late!" Mum yelled up the stairs.
    "I'm coming!" I replied.

    b) "Hello. How can I help you?" the doctor asked.
    "I have a nasty cough and a very sore throat," I replied.

    c) "What would you like in your lunch box tomorrow?" Dad asked.
    "Please can I have ham sandwiches with tomatoes and crisps?" I answered.
    "Of course you can."

    d) "Has everyone got a piece of paper?" Mr Evans asked.
    "I haven't," I said.
    "Don't worry! I will get you one," he replied.

Pages 64–65

1. Little Red Riding Hood skipped out of her house and ran through the forest to her grandma's house. While she was running, she saw some beautiful flowers and stopped to pick some.

    When she arrived at her grandma's house, she went straight into the bedroom, but something was wrong. Little Red Riding Hood thought her grandma looked very strange today.

2. **Accept any three clear and grammatically correct paragraphs.**

Pages 66–67

1. Ouch!
    Where are you?
    I like drinking milk.
    (*1 mark* for all three correct)

2. When we went to the farm, I saw cows, hens, sheep, geese and ducks. (*1 mark for all three correct*)

7

Answers

3. a) **L**isa won first prize in a colouring competition**. S**he was very happy**.** *(1 mark for the two capital letters, 1 mark for the two full stops)*
    b) **I** love cooking with my mum**. W**hen **I** am older, **I** would like to be a chef**.** *(1 mark for the four capital letters, 1 mark for the two full stops)*
4. Is it Wednesday today? *(1 mark)*
5. **Accept any question that is grammatically correct and uses a question mark.** *(1 mark)*
6. **Accept any sentence that is grammatically correct and uses an exclamation mark.** *(1 mark)*
7. Inverted commas *(1 mark)*
8. a) Darcey, Elizabeth, Tom, France. *(1 mark)*
    b) It is a proper noun. *(1 mark)*
9. "Is anyone there?" shouted Mia. *(1 mark)*
10. **"**Can I go and play at Toby's house, please**?"** I asked Mum**.**
    Mum replied**, "**Of course you can**."**
    (1 mark for each correct sentence)
11. When the writing changes time, action, event, place or person. *(2 marks for any two from this list)*

Pages 68–71

1. **D**avid hit the ball so hard it smashed a window**.** *(1 mark)*
2. The birds swooped and darted through the sky. *(1 mark)*
3. Ouch, I've hurt my finger! – Exclamation
    I need a plaster. – Statement
    My finger is bleeding. – Statement
    (1 mark for all three correct)
4. **Any suitable adjective, e.g.:** rough, blue, fierce, etc. *(1 mark)*
5.
singular	plural
car	**cars**
mouse	mice
knife	**knives**

    (1 mark for all 3 correct)

6. a) **an** elephant b) **a** frog
    (1 mark for both correct)
7. a) At the weekend I go swimming**,** play football**,** see friends and watch TV.
    (1 mark)
    b) September**,** April**,** June and November all have thirty days.
    (1 mark)
8. because *(1 mark)*
9. a) The children **were** dancing./The **child** was dancing. *(1 mark)*
    b) Mike **was** laughing. *(1 mark)*
10. I **will ask** for more. *(1 mark)*
11. a, e, i *(1 mark)*
12. **Accept any two clear and grammatically correct questions, e.g.:**
    a) How long did it take to write your book?
    (1 mark)
    b) Who is your favourite character in the story? *(1 mark)*
13. library, books *(1 mark for both correct answers)*
14. gracefully *(1 mark)*
15. **Any suitable adverb, e.g.** clumsily, awkwardly, nicely, etc. *(1 mark)*
16. Jake and **I** watched his dad wash the car.
    (1 mark)
    "You splashed **me**!" I shouted. *(1 mark)*
17. she *(1 mark)*
18. in *(1 mark)*
19. "I like your new glasses," Jamie said.
    "Thank you!" replied Michelle.
    (1 mark for both correct)
20. "You shouldn't feed the animals," the zookeeper said. *(1 mark)*
21. Charlie cycled to school this morning **although** usually he walks. *(1 mark)*

Adjectives 2

3. Now read the same paragraph and fill in the gaps with some **new** adjectives.

Yesterday, we went to the _____ fair. It was _____. There were _____, flashing lights and there was very _____ music. I liked the _____ rides the best. The scariest ride was the ghost train, so I went on that with my _____ dad. At the end of the _____ day, we shared some warm, _____ doughnuts and bought some _____, _____ candyfloss to take home.

4. Rewrite these sentences using adjectives to make your writing more exciting.

   a) The teacher stood in the playground.

   _____
   _____

   b) The firefighter put out the fire.

   _____
   _____

5. Fill in the blanks with adjectives of your choice.

Today was brilliant as it was our school's sports day! The _____ field was covered in _____ balls, bats, _____ skipping ropes, _____ bean bags and many more _____ games. Our class was split into four teams. I was in the _____ team! Lots of _____ mums and dads were sitting on _____ chairs, waiting for us to start our activities and races. When the _____ whistle blew, we were off. Ready, steady, go!

Adverbs 1

Key to grammar

Adverbs describe a verb. Adverbs tell us **how**, **when** or **where** something happens or is done.

> James **quickly** ate his tea.

Adverbs often end with the suffix **ly**. Adverbs that don't end in **ly** include many **when** or **where** adverbs. For example:
- He **sometimes** read. (**when**)
- He read **inside**. (**where**)

Practice activities

1. Look at the sentences below. Circle the adverb(s) in each one.
    a) The artist painted the flower slowly.
    b) The dragon roared fiercely and blew fire out of his nose.
    c) The children shouted loudly in the playground.
    d) Patiently, the audience waited for the show to begin.
    e) Carefully and gently, the nurse bandaged his leg.
    f) The wasp flew angrily around our food.

2. Complete the table below with adverbs that can be used to describe each verb.

talk	run	drink	dance

Adverbs 1

3. Read the passage below. Underline all the adverbs that show **how** the verb is done.

   At my birthday party, there was a clever magician who waved his wand gently over a special box. He shouted the magic words loudly three times, then asked for a helper from the audience. Excitedly, I put up my hand, and before I could change my mind, the magician had chosen me. I went bravely to the front of the stage and helped him mysteriously produce a floppy-eared, soft, white rabbit. Everyone loved the trick and clapped enthusiastically at the end.

4. Choose one of the adverbs from the box below to add to each sentence.

sometimes	Before	Yesterday	outside

   a) _____ they started, the players warmed up.

   b) I _____ fall out with my brother.

   c) I like playing _____ on the trampoline.

   d) _____ it was my birthday.

5. Put a circle around the adverb that fits best in each sentence.

   a) **Soon / Never** it will be summer.

   b) The children giggled **loudly / carefully**.

   c) The teacher **busily / warmly** marked the children's work.

   d) **Perhaps / Never** you could come to my house for tea?

Adverbs 2

Key to grammar

An **adverbial phrase** is a group of words that act like an adverb, giving more information about **how**, **when**, **where** or **why** something is done. For example:
- Clara jumped **into the water.** *(tells us **where**)*
- We have been **at this school for five years**. *(tells us **where** and **when**)*

Fronted adverbials are when an adverb or adverbial phrase has been moved to the **beginning** of a sentence. They are used to create effect and make writing more interesting. A comma is used after a fronted adverbial.

Carefully, the cat walked along the roof.

In 1948, they were married.

Practice activities

1. Read the sentences below and underline the adverbial phrases.

    a) On Friday, I walked for half an hour.

    b) I met my friends outside school.

    c) I usually go and visit my grandma on a Wednesday.

    d) Dan ate some chocolate after his tea.

    e) Kosha practised playing the violin every day.

Adverbs 2

2. Read the sentences below and write whether the adverbial phrases are showing **where**, **when** or **how often** something happens. Some sentences may have more than one answer.

   a) I have a shower every day. _____

   b) My brother hid his homework under his bed. _____

   c) The dog barked when he went for a walk. _____

   d) I go to the library on a Wednesday afternoon. _____

   e) Our English lesson was in the hall. _____

3. Rewrite these sentences putting the adverb at the **front** of the sentence.

   a) The horse galloped quickly down the track.
   _____

   b) The bird darted swiftly through the sky.
   _____

   c) The little girl stroked the purring cat gently.
   _____

   d) The gymnast flew gracefully through the air.
   _____

4. Write a fronted adverbial phrase of your own.
   _____

Determiners

Key to grammar

A **determiner** stands before a noun or a word that describes the noun (an adjective). The most common determiners are **the**, **a** and **an**.

Before a word beginning with a consonant sound we use **a**, but before a word beginning with a vowel sound we use **an** (sometimes **h** at the start of a word can be silent, so we use **an** rather than **a**).

a spider   **a** hotel   **an** octopus   **an** hour

Practice activities

1. Underline the determiners in each sentence.

    a) The girl put on a jumper.

    b) I need a paint brush.

    c) I had an egg for breakfast.

2. Fill the table below with words that would follow **a** or **an**. Two have been added to the table already, as examples.

a	an
boy	egg

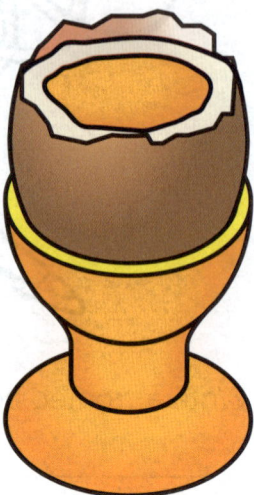

42

Determiners

3. Read the words below and decide whether to use **a** or **an**.

    a) _____ trumpet   b) _____ elephant

    c) _____ umbrella   d) _____ game

    e) _____ holiday   f) _____ insect

4. Choose **a**, **an** or **the** to fill in the gaps in the sentences below.

    a) I need to wear _____ sunhat when _____ sun is shining.

    b) I saw _____ ant crawling along _____ leaves.

    c) When I go to _____ shops, I need to buy _____ loaf of bread.

    d) _____ teacher read _____ story in assembly this morning.

    e) Alicia had _____ tummy ache after eating too many cakes.

5. Rewrite these sentences correctly, replacing **a**, **an** or **the** with the correct word.

    a) Paige likes reading an book about dinosaurs.

    _____

    b) I will be back in a hour.

    _____

    c) A animals were waiting to see the vet.

    _____

43

Conjunctions

Key to grammar

Conjunctions are connecting words. They link words, phrases, clauses or sentences.

Some common conjunctions are:

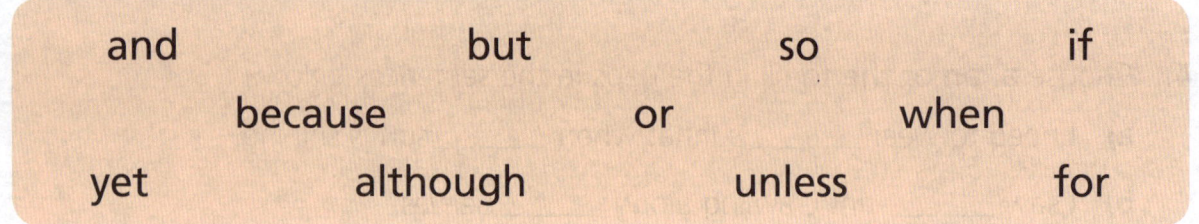

and	but	so	if
because	or	when	
yet	although	unless	for

You must take your shoes off **so** you don't get dirt on the carpet.

We need to wash our hands **because** it is nearly dinner time.

Although Missy was only small, she had a very loud bark!

Practice activities

1. Underline the conjunctions in the sentences.

    a) I like oranges, but my sister prefers apples.

    b) I am feeling cold and I have a headache.

    c) My dad said I could have a new bike if I keep my bedroom tidy.

    d) We have a different teacher today because Mrs Power is ill.

Conjunctions

2. Choose the correct conjunction from the box below to add to the sentences.

   | because | and | so | but | unless |

   a) _____ I feel better tomorrow, I will need to see a doctor.

   b) The baby cried _____ he was hungry.

   c) It is raining, _____ I will need to put on my coat.

   d) I like eating chocolate, _____ Natasha prefers ice cream!

   e) We are going to the cinema _____ we are going to buy some popcorn.

3. Write sentences using the conjunctions in brackets.

   a) (**because**) _____

   _____

   b) (**so**) _____

   _____

   c) (**or**) _____

   _____

   d) (**unless**) _____

   _____

   e) (**when**) _____

   _____

Time connectives

Key to grammar

Time connectives are used to show the passing of time. They link words and sentences together to show the order in which events happen or have happened.

Here are some examples:

> by the time   since   when   finally
> as soon as   before   next   then
> after   later   firstly   meanwhile   eventually

Practice activities

1. Underline the time connectives in the sentences.

    a) I need to be at school before nine o'clock.

    b) When I make a cake, I read the recipe. Next, I find the ingredients I need.

    c) "You can go outside to play as soon as it has stopped raining," my mum said.

    d) Mr Bull helped our class learn some new songs, then he helped another class.

    e) We have been waiting for the bus to arrive since nine o'clock.

    f) My birthday is in June, then it will be Amy's in July.

    g) When the plane finally arrived in Spain, I was feeling very excited.

Time connectives

2. Look at the instructions below for baking a cake. Choose a time connective from the box and write it in the correct place.

as soon as	First	Finally		
	Meanwhile	then	Next	When

a) _____, weigh the ingredients.

b) _____, put the sugar and butter in a bowl and mix well.

c) Add two eggs and stir carefully, _____ add sieved flour.

d) Fold the flour into the mixture and _____ the flour is well mixed, pour the mixture into the cake tin.

e) _____ the mixture is in the cake tin, put it into the oven for forty minutes.

f) _____, tidy the kitchen and wash the bowls.

g) _____, take the cake out of the oven and let it cool.

3. Write sentences using the connectives in brackets.

a) (**next**) _____

_____

b) (**then**) _____

_____

c) (**as soon as**) _____

_____

Test your grammar

These questions will help you to practise the grammar skills you have learned in this book. They will also help you prepare for the grammar and punctuation test that you will take in Year 6 at the end of Key Stage 2.

Make sure you read each question carefully and do what it asks. The questions slowly get harder to help you progress steadily.

1. Draw a line to match the words to the correct sentence structure.

Oh no!		question
Where are you going?		statement
The sea was very cold.		exclamation

   1 mark

2. Circle the **verb** in this sentence.

   Mum put on her shoes quickly.

   1 mark

3. Look at the table below. Fill in the gaps.

Present tense	Past tense
play	
	swam
	laughed
build	
run	
	cried
fall	

   2 marks

48

Test your grammar

4. Underline the **superlative adjective** in this sentence

The smartest dog won first prize in the dog show last night. *1 mark*

5. Which sentence contains **two adverbs**?

Tick **one**

Slowly the car pulled away down the winding driveway. ☐

Emily danced gracefully at the party. ☐

Cautiously and carefully, Sam lifted the cakes out of the oven. ☐

The dog ate the food hungrily and then looked for more. ☐

1 mark

6. Read the sentence below and circle all the **nouns**.

I rode on my bike while my cousin rode his scooter. *1 mark*

7. Read the sentence below. Choose the most suitable **pronoun** to fill the gap.

Jessica went to the theatre and _____ watched a play.

she   **her**   **it**   **me**   *1 mark*

8. Circle the **conjunction** in the sentence below.

Lucy was feeling excited because it was her birthday tomorrow. *1 mark*

9. In which sentence do the **subject** and **verb** agree?

Tick **one**

Most of my friends likes drinking lemonade. ☐

Girls is reading books in the library. ☐

Everyone is going to the cinema tonight. ☐

The dog live in the kennels. ☐

The man swim in the sea. ☐

1 mark

10. Underline the **main clause** in this sentence.

When they were young, the children loved going camping. *1 mark*

11. Write this sentence in the **present perfect tense**.

I did all my homework. *1 mark*

_____

Full stops

Key to punctuation

Most sentences end with a **full stop**.

Tom went into the library to borrow a book.

This morning, I decided to bake a cake. I had to go to the shops to buy the ingredients.

Practice activities

1. Read the sentences below and put full stops in the correct places.

    a) I am going to go to After School Club today

    b) The farmer has lots of animals in his field

    c) We are going to the seaside tomorrow I am looking forward to it

    d) "Help! Help!" they shouted The children were stuck inside the shed They couldn't get out

2. Look at the pictures and write **one sentence** about each one. Do not forget to use a full stop.

    a)

    b)

Full stops

3. Goldilocks has forgotten to use full stops in her letter to the Three Bears. Read the letter then add the full stops in the correct places.

> *Dear Daddy Bear, Mummy Bear and Baby Bear,*
>
> *I am so sorry that I broke into your house I was very hungry and could see your lovely bowls of porridge cooling on the table Baby Bear, your porridge was delicious It tasted just right*
>
> *After eating all the porridge, I decided to have a rest I didn't mean to break the chair in your living room I didn't know what to do, so I went upstairs and hid I loved Baby Bear's bed It was so comfy! I must have fallen asleep before you came back You seemed very cross with me so I ran out of your cottage and hid further down the path I didn't want to get into trouble*
>
> *I hope one day you will forgive me and we can be friends*
>
> *Lots of love,*
>
> *Goldilocks xxx*

4. The Three Bears have replied to Goldilocks but they have put the full stops in the wrong places. Rewrite their letter below, putting the full stops in correctly.

> *Dear Goldilocks,*
>
> *Thank you. for your letter We accept your apology. and hope we can now be friends Would. you like to come round to our cottage. again sometime? Maybe we could. cook you some. tea. Baby Bear would love to play. with you in the garden Please let us know. if you would like that. too.*
>
> *Lots of love,*
>
> *The Three Bears xxx*

Exclamation marks

Key to punctuation

An **exclamation mark** can be used at the end of a command to show it is urgent. For example:
- Go away**!**
- Quick, run**!**

An exclamation mark can also be used at the end of a sentence to show emotion, such as happiness, excitement, pain or anger. For example:
- How wonderful**!**
- That's a disgrace**!**

Practice activities

1. Read this story about the Gingerbread Man and add **nine** exclamation marks in the correct places.

   Once upon a time, there was a little old lady and a little old man. One day, they decided to bake a gingerbread man, so they made him carefully and then put him in the oven to cook.

   When the Gingerbread Man was ready, the little old lady opened the oven door, but, … oh, no The Gingerbread Man ran away Before the little old man and the little old lady had blinked, the Gingerbread Man had run out of the house and was halfway up the road.

   " Run, run as fast as you can You can't catch me. I'm the Gingerbread Man "

   " Help " cried the little old lady to a nearby farmer.

   " Quick, run " shouted the farmer, " We can catch him "

   But the Gingerbread Man continued to run, still singing. " Run, run as fast as you can You can't catch me. I'm the Gingerbread Man "

Exclamation marks

2. Look at the exclamations and write a sentence after each one. Do not forget to include an exclamation mark.

Example: Oh, no!

    Oh, no! My toast is burnt!

a) **Ouch!**

_____

b) **Stop it!**

_____

c) **Don't touch!**

_____

d) **Quick, run!**

_____

e) **Help!**

_____

3. Draw lines to match each exclamation with its correct description.

Ouch!	an order
Wow!	pain
Go away!	surprise

Question marks

Key to punctuation

A **question mark** is used at the end of a sentence when a question is being asked. A question mark is used instead of a full stop.

Are you ready to order?

Practice activities

1. Read the questions below. Put a question mark in the correct place.

    a) Please can someone help me

    b) Would you like to go to the playground today

    c) Where is the train station

2. Read the sentences below. Decide which ones are questions and which ones are statements and then put either a question mark or a full stop in the correct place.

    a) I am going outside to play in the snow

    b) Are you ready for the race tomorrow

    c) Which colour do you prefer

    d) Where are my shoes I can't find them anywhere

    e) The children were excited about the school disco

Question marks

3. Look at the pictures of London.

Write questions about the pictures starting with the different question words below. Do not forget to end each question with a question mark.

Example: Could we catch the bus?

a) Where _____

b) When _____

c) How _____

d) What _____

e) Which _____

f) Have _____

Capital letters

Key to punctuation

A capital letter is used at the **start** of every sentence.

A **capital letter** is also always used at the start of a **proper noun** (the name of something or someone) and for the pronoun **I**.

Mary

December

Australia

Proper nouns and the pronoun **I** always start with a capital letter, even if they are in the middle of a sentence.

Practice activities

1. a) Look at the nouns below.

Put a circle around the ones that should start with a capital letter.

december   **paul**   **shop**

seaside   **cat**

france   **david**   **garden**

b) Write the nouns you have circled in part a), using a capital letter.

i) _____   ii) _____

iii) _____   iv) _____

Capital letters

2. Read the weather report below.

Put a circle around the letters that should be capital letters.

today will be a warm, dry day. it will start cloudy in most areas of england and wales, but by lunchtime the sun will be shining! devon and cornwall will see the highest temperatures, whereas lincolnshire and yorkshire will be the coolest.

tonight will remain warm and slightly humid, and tomorrow and thursday we may see some heavy thunderstorms.

3. Rewrite the sentences below using capital letters in the correct places.

a) on a monday evening, leah and kate go to choir practice.

b) my birthday is in march, but my sister's birthday is in august.

c) mr thomson's pupils were being very noisy because they were practising a play.

d) pebbles was a shy cat who didn't like mrs stone, the vet.

e) our favourite sport is football. we play it every saturday at the park.

Commas in a list

Key to punctuation

Commas are used to separate words in a list.

In my shopping basket there are eggs, milk and bread.

I like playing tennis, football, cricket and badminton.

The final word in a list is joined to the others with another word (usually **and**) instead of using a comma.

Practice activities

1. Put commas in the correct places in these sentences.

   a) I am wearing trousers a T-shirt socks and shoes.

   b) My favourite colours are red blue green yellow and silver.

   c) My mum can play the piano the flute and the clarinet.

   d) I like playing on the swings slide and roundabout.

   e) My favourite subjects at school are English music science and PE.

   f) My cousins are called Chloe Jules Safa and Joe.

   g) On holiday I went to the beach the swimming pool the disco and the museum.

Commas in a list

2. Some of the commas in the sentences below are in the wrong place or are not needed. Rewrite the sentences placing commas where they are needed.

   a) The fish, is, yellow, blue, green, and, gold.

   _____

   _____

   b) My sandwich, has, ham, cheese, butter, and, pickle in it.

   _____

   _____

3. Use the shopping lists in the boxes to finish the sentences below.

a)	bread	b)	apples	c)	peas
	milk		oranges		carrots
	jam		bananas		broccoli
	eggs		strawberries		celery
	sugar		pears		tomatoes

   a) I would like some _____

   _____

   b) I need _____

   _____

   c) I must remember to buy some _____

   _____

Direct speech 1

Key to punctuation

Direct speech is what a speaker actually says. When we write, we put **inverted commas** around direct speech. These are sometimes known as **speech marks**.

If the sentence begins with direct speech, we add a comma, exclamation mark or question mark just before the closing inverted commas and then usually let the reader know who said it.

"I wish I could go to the ball," Cinderella said.

If the sentence begins by telling us who is speaking, a comma should appear before the speech begins. When the direct speech finishes, it should normally end with a full stop, question mark or exclamation mark just before the closing inverted commas.

The Fairy Godmother replied, "You shall go to the ball!"

Practice activities

1. Put inverted commas around what is being said below.

    a) Sweep the floors and iron our clothes, Cinderella! shouted the Ugly Sisters.

    b) Hurry up with the washing, Cinderella!

    c) Cinderella whispered to herself, I would love to wear a pretty dress.

Direct speech 1

2. Put inverted commas and punctuation in the correct places in the sentences below.

   a) How long is it until dinner is ready   Sam asked

   b) What time do you usually go to bed

   c) Please can I go to the park, Mum   Rachel asked

   d) Oh no   sighed Dad

   e) Where would you like to go on holiday   Mum and Dad asked

   f) The man next door shouted   Keep the noise down, please

   g) The teacher shouted   Sit down everyone

   h) Have you eaten all your dinner today   Mum asked

3. Rewrite these sentences adding inverted commas in the correct place.

   a) What time does your party start? Olivia asked.

   b) Can I have a drink of water, please? Radi asked his teacher.

   c) Go and put your shoes on! Mum shouted.

Direct speech 2

Key to punctuation

In a conversation between two or more people, when a new person starts speaking, the speech is written on a **new line**.

"Please can I have some new rollerblades?" I asked my mum hopefully.

Mum replied, "You will have to wait until it is your birthday."

"But that is ages away!"

"You could save your pocket money," Mum suggested, "and buy some yourself."

Notice that all direct speech starts with a **capital letter**, except where the sentence of direct speech is broken by information about who is talking.

N.B. **inverted commas** are also called speech marks.

Practice activities

1. Put inverted commas around what is being said in these sentences.
    a) I love going to school, Ben said.
    b) The train is delayed, so I'm going to be home late, Dad grumbled.
    c) Can you tell me where the nearest shop is, please?
    d) Ouch! Mrs Baker shouted. I've hurt my toe!

Direct speech 2

2. Add inverted commas and the correct punctuation to these sentences.

  a) What time are you leaving I asked my friends

  b) We will be going at about two o'clock they replied

  c) Can I come too I asked

  d) Of course you can

3. Rewrite these conversations using inverted commas and the correct punctuation. Remember to start a new line for each new speaker.

  a) Hurry up You'll be late Mum yelled up the stairs I'm coming I replied

  b) Hello How can I help you the doctor asked I have a nasty cough and a very sore throat I replied

  c) What would you like in your lunch box tomorrow Dad asked Please can I have ham sandwiches with tomatoes and crisps I answered Of course you can.

  d) Has everyone got a piece of paper Mr Evans asked I haven't I said Don't worry I will get you one he replied.

Paragraphs

Key to punctuation

Paragraphs are groups of sentences that are related to each other. A paragraph often has sentences in it about the same thing or point. A new paragraph is usually started when the writing changes to a new time, action, event, place or person. Usually, a new paragraph starts on a new line and is **indented** (a small gap is left to show that a new paragraph is starting). However, paragraphs are sometimes separated by a **line space** and are not indented.

Indented paragraph

...so snatching up all his things and without stopping to think, Imran bolted out of the door.

   When he got to the end of the lane and could see clearly down the high street, he saw what looked like...

Line-spaced paragraph

... so snatching up all his things and without stopping to think, Imran bolted out of the door.

When he got to the end of the lane and could see clearly down the high street, he saw what looked like...

Practice activities

1. Read the extract below and place a tick where you think a new paragraph could begin.

   Little Red Riding Hood skipped out of her house and ran through the forest to her grandma's house. While she was running, she saw some beautiful flowers and stopped to pick some. When she arrived at her grandma's house, she went straight into the bedroom, but something was wrong. Little Red Riding Hood thought her grandma looked very strange today.

Paragraphs

2. Look at the basic facts below, which have been taken from a newspaper report. Then make up your own newspaper article using a separate paragraph for each fact.

Animals escaped from the zoo.

The zoo had to close.

The police were called.

Test your punctuation

These questions will help you to practise the punctuation skills you have learned in this book. They will also help you prepare for the grammar and punctuation test that you will take in Year 6 at the end of Key Stage 2.

Make sure you read each question carefully and do what it asks. The questions slowly get harder to help you progress steadily.

1. Draw a line to match each group of words to the correct punctuation mark.

Ouch	?
Where are you	.
I like drinking milk	!

   1 mark

2. Add **three** more commas in the right places to make this sentence correct.

   When we went to the farm, I saw cows hens sheep geese and ducks.

   1 mark

3. Read the sentences below. Put a circle around any letters that should be **capital letters**, and add the **full stops**.

   a) lisa won first prize in a colouring competition she was very happy

   b) i love cooking with my mum when i am older, i would like to be a chef

   2 marks

4. Which sentence is punctuated correctly?

   Tick one

   Is it Wednesday today? ☐
   Is it Wednesday today. ☐
   Is it Wednesday today! ☐
   Is it Wednesday today, ☐

   1 mark

5. Write a **question**.

   _____

   1 mark

Test your punctuation

6. Write an **exclamation**.

_____

1 mark

7. What type of punctuation is another name for **speech marks**?

Tick **one**

commas ☐

exclamation marks ☐

inverted full stops ☐

inverted commas ☐

1 mark

8. Put a circle around the words that should start with a **capital letter**.

   a) darcey, elizabeth and tom went to france on a school trip.

1 mark

   b) Pick **one** of the words you have circled and explain why it needs a capital letter.

   _____

   _____

1 mark

9. Add **inverted commas** in the correct place to this sentence.

Is anyone there? shouted Mia.

1 mark

10. Add the **inverted commas** and **correct punctuation** to this conversation.

Can I go and play at Toby's house, please I asked Mum

Mum replied Of course you can

2 marks

11. Give **two** reasons why a new paragraph should be started.

_____

_____

2 marks

Mixed test

These questions give you another chance to practise the grammar and punctuation skills you have learned in this book. They will also help you prepare for the grammar and punctuation test that you will take in Year 6 at the end of Key Stage 2.

Make sure you read each question carefully and do what it asks. The questions slowly get harder to help you progress steadily.

1. Copy the sentence below. Add any missing **full stops** or **capital letters**.

    david hit the ball so hard it smashed a window

    _____

    _____

    1 mark

2. Which sentence contains **two verbs**?

    Tick **one**

The birds flew in the sky.	☐
The birds flew down to their nests.	☐
The birds swooped and darted through the sky.	☐
The birds collected worms.	☐

    1 mark

3. Put a tick in each row to show whether the sentence is a statement or an exclamation.

Sentence	Statement	Exclamation
Ouch, I've hurt my finger!		
I need a plaster.		
My finger is bleeding.		

    1 mark

Mixed test

4. Complete the sentence below with an **adjective** that makes sense.

The _____ sea crashed against the rocks. *1 mark*

5. Complete the table to show the singular and plural forms of each noun.

Singular	Plural
car	
	mice
knife	

1 mark

6. Write either **a** or **an** before each noun.

   a) _____ elephant

   b) _____ frog   *1 mark*

7. Put commas in the correct places to separate the items in the lists.

   a) At the weekend I go swimming play football see friends and watch TV.

   b) September April June and November all have thirty days.

2 marks

8. Circle the **conjunction** in this sentence.

The children needed a wash because they were dirty. *1 mark*

9. The sentences below are incorrect. Rewrite them correctly.

   a) The children was dancing. _____

   b) Mike were laughing. _____

2 marks

10. Change this sentence to the **future tense**.

I asked for more.

_____

1 mark

69

Mixed test

11. Put a circle around the **vowels**.

    s   t   h   a   e   l   m   p   w   i   *1 mark*

12. Write two questions you would like to ask an author.

    a) _____

    b) _____

    2 marks

13. Read the sentence and circle all the **nouns**.

    I like going to the library and choosing new books.   *1 mark*

14. Circle the **adverb** in this sentence.

    The ballerina danced gracefully in her exam this morning.   *1 mark*

15. Write a **different adverb** to change the meaning of the sentence.

    The ballerina danced _____ in her exam this morning.   *1 mark*

16. Add the pronouns **I** and **me** to the sentences below to make them correct.

    Jake and _____ watched his dad wash the car.

    "You splashed _____ !" I shouted.   *2 marks*

17. Choose a **pronoun** from the words below to complete the sentence.

    Aisha went to the shops and _____ bought some ice cream.

    her   **she**   **we**   **it**   **me**   *1 mark*

18. Which **preposition** would fit best in this sentence?

    The car is _____ the garage.

    Tick **one**

out	☐
round	☐
over	☐
in	☐

1 mark

Mixed test

19. Put **inverted commas** in the correct place in the sentences below.

I like your new glasses, Jamie said.

Thank you! replied Michelle.

1 mark

20. Which sentence uses **inverted commas** and **commas** correctly?

Tick **one**

"You shouldn't feed the animals," the zookeeper said. ☐

"You shouldn't feed the animals, the zookeeper said." ☐

"You shouldn't feed the animals" the zookeeper, said. ☐

You shouldn't feed the animals, "the zookeeper said." ☐

1 mark

21. Circle the most suitable connective to complete the sentence below.

Charlie cycled to school this morning _____ usually he walks.

because **although** **and** **next** *1 mark*

Acknowledgements

The author and publisher are grateful to the copyright holders for permission to use quoted materials and images.

All images are ©Shutterstock, ©Jupiterimages, ©Clipart.com or ©Letts Educational, an imprint of HarperCollins*Publishers* Ltd

Every effort has been made to trace copyright holders and obtain their permission for the use of copyright material. The author and publisher will gladly receive information enabling them to rectify any error or omission in subsequent editions. All facts are correct at time of going to press.

Published by Letts Educational
An imprint of HarperCollins*Publishers* Ltd
1 London Bridge Street
London SE1 9GF

ISBN 9780008294205

First published 2013

This edition published 2018

10 9 8 7 6 5 4 3 2 1

© 2018 Letts Educational, an imprint of HarperCollins*Publishers* Ltd

All rights reserved. No part of this publication may be reproduced, stored in a retrieval system, or transmitted, in any form or by any means, electronic, mechanical, photocopying, recording or otherwise, without the prior permission of Letts Educational.

British Library Cataloguing in Publication Data.

A CIP record of this book is available from the British Library.

Commissioning Editor: Tammy Poggo

Author: Laura Griffiths

Project Editors: Daniel Dyer and Charlotte Christensen

Cover Design: Paul Oates

Inside Concept Design: Ian Wrigley

Layout: Jouve India Private Limited

Production: Natalia Rebow

Printed and bound by Bell and Bain Ltd, Glasgow

MIX
Paper from responsible sources
FSC C007454